Seeds of Change

Seeds of Change

THE GREEN REVOLUTION AND DEVELOPMENT IN THE 1970's

Lester R. Brown

Foreword by
Eugene R. Black

PUBLISHED FOR THE OVERSEAS DEVELOPMENT COUNCIL

BY

PRAEGER PUBLISHERS
New York · Washington · London

PRAEGER PUBLISHERS
111 Fourth Avenue, New York, N.Y. 10003, U.S.A.
5, Cromwell Place, London S.W.7, England

Published in the United States of America in 1970
by Praeger Publishers, Inc.

© 1970 by Praeger Publishers, Inc.

Library of Congress Catalog Card Number: 77–109015

Printed in the United States of America

Contents

18079

Foreword

By EUGENE R. BLACK

Where development is concerned, the first requirement is change, and change in human affairs never comes easy. This is a book about change. The agricultural breakthrough in the poor countries, the Green Revolution, is the most exciting development story of the past decade. The new "miracle" rice and wheat seeds are proving to be engines of change on a vast scale. They bring hope, enabling us to raise our sights as to what might be accomplished in international development during the 'seventies.

Mr. Brown's emphasis on the potential of the Green Revolution is not surprising. Appointed head of USDA's International Agricultural Development Service at age 32, he was one of the architects of the policies that permitted the United States to play a key role in launching the Green Revolution. As an economic phenomenon, the food-production breakthrough in the poor countries rivals the postwar reconstruction of Europe. America's participation in this revolution in the countryside may represent our most successful involvement in international development since the Marshall Plan.

The principal contribution of this book is its statement of the alternatives open to us as a result of this historic breakthrough. Skillfully handled in the 'seventies, the Green Revolution can become the vehicle for eliminating most of the malnutrition and hunger that now cripple half the people on this planet and for providing millions of new jobs in the countryside. Poorly managed, the new seeds and their associated technologies could displace millions in the countryside, forcing them into the already overcrowded cities.

The future will determine whether the prospects of the breakthrough in food production are realized, but the story must be told now, for there is a crisis in international-development cooperation today. This crisis is born of unrealistic expectations in the past, dispute over the Vietnam war, and new preoccupations here at home which have siphoned off much of the humanitarian energy that used to be devoted to what we call our foreign-aid programs. Although I have never liked the phrase "foreign aid," preferring to talk about development finance, I am concerned about this crisis. People the world over look to Americans to sustain their confidence in the possibilities of development. If we waver, they will, too.

Lester Brown writes about an important set of options open to us as we consider the nature of future United States involvement in the global development effort. The first purpose of the Overseas Development Council, of which I am chairman and Mr. Brown is a Senior Fellow, is to identify these issues of development and to stimulate discussion of them among interested people and organizations. The Council, which at present has the support of 33 business corporations and 13 foundations, made the publication of this book possible. I regard *Seeds of Change* as "must" reading for all those who believe, as I do, that our participation in world development must continue and must become the distinguishing feature of our efforts to help keep the peace.

Preface

Achieving an acceptable balance between food and people is widely regarded as one of the two most difficult problems facing mankind in the remaining third of the twentieth century. The other is averting nuclear war. Advances in weapons technology and the continuing arms race may actually be increasing the risk of the latter, but technological breakthroughs in agriculture are making the food-population problem appear much more manageable. Dramatic successes in raising food output in the poor countries are beginning to dispel the gloomy forecasts of widespread famine and worsening hunger.

This book tells the story of the turnaround on the food front. Its heroes are new high-yielding cereals and the men who developed them. These new seeds are triggering an agricultural revolution in poor countries such as Pakistan, India, Turkey, the Philippines, Kenya, and Mexico, a revolution that makes the earlier agricultural takeoffs in the United States and Japan seem minor by comparison.

I am fortunate to have had a front-row seat in this historic drama. Beginning in 1964, I worked with Secretary of Agriculture Orville L. Freeman as adviser on foreign agricultural policy. From 1966 to 1969 I also served as Administrator of the International Development Service, the technical-assistance arm of the Department.

My own interest in the food problem runs deep. Born and reared on a farm in southern New Jersey, I organized, at the age of 14, a commercial tomato-growing operation with my younger brother, an operation that was to see me through college. Six months spent living in Indian villages in 1956 broadened my interest in global agriculture by exposing me to a way of life typical of the vast majority of mankind, the peasant farmers in the poor countries. This interest led me to join the Department of Agriculture in 1959.

Under the leadership of Secretary Freeman, the Department assumed global responsibilities for food aid and agricultural technical assistance. The Secretary, following a long line of American farmer-politicians, regarded the farmers of the world as his constituents and tried to bring them something of the knowledge that has made farming in the United States the skilled profession it is today.

As the 'sixties progressed, we in the Department became increasingly concerned over the growing imbalance in the food-population equation. In the spring of 1965 I prepared a report for the Secretary on *Increasing World Food Output* that began with the statement: "The less developed world is losing the capacity to feed itself."

The gap between food production and consumption in the poor countries was widening. Famine had been avoided during the postwar period, but only because American farmers were growing more and more food for shipment abroad in food aid—enough, in fact, to feed 100 million people in 1965.

In 1966, the USDA's Economic Research Service prepared its "1984 Graph," which showed that the United States could continue to fill the widening gap only until the end of 1984, after which food needs in the hungry countries would exceed our capacity to respond. This doomsday date was arrived at by projecting historical trends under a series of conservative assumptions.

Others were even more alarmed. Early in 1967, in their book *Famine 1975*, William and Paul Paddock argued that massive famine was inevitable by 1975, nine years earlier than the USDA graph predicted. They urged the United States to identify the countries that had some chance of "making it" and then to concentrate food aid and technical assistance on those countries, abandoning the others.

Also in 1967, the prestigious Science Advisory Committee to the President published a three-volume report on *The World Food Problem,* showing that the rate of growth in food production in the poor countries for the 1960–65 period was scarcely half the rate of population growth. Clearly, population and food trends were on a "collision course."

Dramatic gains in cereal output in the past few years now demand a fresh assessment of the prospects of meeting the future food needs of the poor countries. This book, essentially an expansion of an article which appeared in the July, 1968, issue of *Foreign Affairs,* attempts to provide such an assessment.

James P. Grant, President of the Overseas Development Council, and I chose the breakthrough in agriculture as our first research project for several important reasons. Agriculture is "where the action is" in economic development today. The extensive role of the United States in the agricultural revolution may represent our most successful involvement abroad since the Marshal Plan. And, most important, the agricultural revolution is bringing into focus some of the central questions regarding the future relationship between the rich and poor countries.

This book is written for laymen as well as for those engaged in development. The implications of the new agricultural technologies not only demand attention from a host of different professions; they must be understood by all those whose opinions and actions may affect future plans and political decisions. The potential of the new technologies to alleviate global hunger should make the book of interest to the concerned layman, academician, and humanitarian as well.

The food-production breakthrough demonstrates that man is capable of responding to crises, a fact that many of us, beset with the numerous complex and seemingly insoluble problems of today, were beginning to doubt. This brief volume attempts to outline the potential of the agricultural revolution, the issues emerging from it, and the difficult choices that must be made in the months and years ahead. The wisdom of these choices will determine the extent to which the agricultural revolution fulfills its promise of a better life for that half of the human family living in the rural areas of the poor countries.

LESTER R. BROWN

Washington, D.C.
November, 1969

Acknowledgments

Although this book has only one author, it is, in a sense, the product of a community of interested officials, scholars, and individuals. I bear responsibility for the manuscript, but it has been greatly enriched by the comments of reviewers at various stages in its evolution.

Some twenty individuals have read and reviewed the manuscript. These include my colleagues Colin Bradford and Harald Malmgren; Board members Edward Mason and John Schnittker; from USDA, Aaron Altschul, Jay Atkinson, Dana Dalrymple, Horace Davis, I. M. Destler, Charles Gibbons, William Jones, Martin Kriesberg, Don Paarlberg, Neill Schaller, and Lyle Schertz; from AID, Dale Adams and Frank Parker; from the World Bank, Price Gittinger and Shigeharu Takahashi; George Mehren, of the Agribusiness Council; Phillips Foster, of the University of Maryland; Hans Landsberg, of Resources for the Future; and former Secretary of Agriculture Orville L. Freeman.

Three people must be singled out for their special contributions. James Grant, President of ODC, insisted that the Green Revolution be related to the major issues facing man —hunger, poverty, population growth, unemployment, and the environmental crisis. The manuscript bears the heavy imprint of his hand. Nat McKitterick repeatedly broke the mold of my thinking, forcing me to put the pieces back together again and again until they fit. Nat also helped to improve the style and flow of the writing. Robert Shaw, who labored with me for several months in researching the principal issues addressed in the maunscript, was a great help in clarifying some of the more complex ones.

I hope that SEEDS OF CHANGE will prove to be a useful work, thus providing some compensation to my wife, Shirley Ann, and my children, Brian and Brenda, for the many things we didn't get to do during the months while it was being written.

The Overseas Development Council is dedicated to increasing the American people's understanding of the problems of development of the low-income countries and to the more effective pursuit of that development.

It is concerned with focusing attention and stimulating action on development problems and on the means, public and private, of assisting the development process in these countries, including the role and effectiveness of assistance mechanisms.

In publishing a study, the Council presents it as a competent treatment of a subject worthy of public consideration. The interpretations and conclusions in such publications are those of the author or authors and do not necessarily reflect the views of other members of the Council staff or of the administrative officers of the Council.

Seeds of Change

I

Introduction: The Green Revolution

Late in 1944, a group of four young Americans assembled in the hills outside Mexico City. Their mission was to export the United States agricultural revolution to Mexico. They believed that the application of science to agriculture could achieve the same results in the poor countries as in the United States. Like Mao Tse-tung, they believed that the future of these countries would be decided in the countryside.

The four young revolutionaries were agricultural scientists, the initial staff of an organization assembled and financed by the Rockefeller Foundation at the request of the Mexican government. Their leader, Dr. George Harrar, a young plant pathologist, was later to become President of the Foundation.

When the group arrived in Mexico, it was a hungry country, importing much of its food from the United States. By 1967, only a quarter of a century later, wheat production had tripled, corn production had doubled, and the average Mexican was consuming 40 per cent more food. Both wheat and corn were being exported, and the economy was prospering. At the heart of this agricultural revolution were new high-yielding wheats developed by Dr. Harrar's group and its successors. Widely adapted to conditions in the tropical-sub-tropical countries, these wheats proved capable of doubling yields when properly managed and given sufficient water and fertilizer.

3

Encouraged by its extraordinary successes with wheat in Mexico, the Rockefeller Foundation joined forces with the Ford Foundation in 1962 to establish the International Rice Research Institute at Los Banos, in the Philippines. Building on the Mexican experience, scientists at IRRI, under the leadership of Dr. Robert Chandler, struck pay dirt quickly when one of their early crosses produced a prolific dwarf rice, IR-8, now known around the world as the "miracle rice." Like the Mexican wheats, IR-8 was capable of doubling yields, given the appropriate management and inputs.

THE SPREAD OF THE REVOLUTION

For most readers of this book, the outstanding technological achievement of this generation was the recent landing on the moon by astronauts Armstrong and Aldrin. But for the one billion Asians for whom rice is the staple food, the development of IR-8 and its dissemination throughout Asia is a more meaningful achievement. It is literally helping to fill hundreds of millions of rice bowls once only half full. For those for whom hunger is a way of life, technology can offer no greater reward. Population growth and food production in this region, containing more than half the world's people, were on a collision course. Although hunger and severe malnutrition persist, today the prospect of widespread famine is receding.

Between 1965 and 1969, land planted to the new varieties of wheat and rice in Asia expanded from 200 acres to 34 million acres, roughly one tenth of the region's total grain acreage. In one of the most spectacular advances in cereal production ever recorded by any country, Pakistan increased its wheat harvest nearly 60 per cent between 1967 and 1969. This brought Pakistan, as recently as 1967 the second largest recipient of United States food aid, to the brink of cereal self-sufficiency. Progress for Pakistan is not limited to wheat, for its record rice harvest in 1968 eliminated its deficit in rice, bringing it into the world market as a net exporter in 1969.

India's production of wheat, expanding much faster than the other cereals, climbed 50 per cent between 1965 and 1969. Assuming political stability, present estimates indicate that India should be able to feed her vast and growing population from her own resources by 1972.

Ceylon's rice crop has increased 34 per cent in the past two years. The Philippines, with four consecutive record rice harvests, has ended a half century of dependence on rice imports, becoming a rice exporter. Among the other Asian countries that are beginning to benefit from the new seeds are Turkey, Burma, Malaysia, Indonesia, and Vietnam. Even such remotely situated Asian countries as Afghanistan, Nepal, and Laos are using the new seeds.

Before the introduction of the new seeds into the region, the stork was fast outrunning the plow.

Although the most dramatic gains thus far are concentrated in Asia, countries elsewhere are also beginning to capitalize on the new cereals. Kenya, in East Africa, and the Ivory Coast, in West Africa, have turned in impressive agricultural performances in recent years. Kenya is now exporting corn, and rice production in the Ivory Coast more than doubled during the 'sixties. The Mexican wheats, introduced recently in Tunisia and Morocco, are beginning to spread in both countries. Algeria and Libya imported large supplies of the new wheat seeds in 1969. Brazil and Paraguay each achieved dramatic gains in wheat production in 1968.

The new seeds, of course, do not provide an ultimate solution to the food-population problem. The collision between population growth and food production has been averted only temporarily. But the new seeds have bought time in which to seek a breakthrough in contraception comparable to the breakthrough in plant breeding.

PREPARING THE GROUND

The word "revolution" has been greatly abused, but no other term adequately describes the effects of the new seeds on the poor countries where they are being used. The technological breakthrough achieved by agricultural scientists foreshadows widespread changes in the economic, social, and political orders of the poor countries.

Had the high-yielding seeds been developed a decade earlier, however, it is doubtful that a revolution would have occurred. A decade ago planners and politicians in the poor countries favored industry to the neglect of agriculture. Even though international cooperation in agricultural development was well established, it was only beginning to result in the kind of infrastructure—farm-to-market roads, experimental stations, fertilizer distribution systems, irrigation schemes, credit and extension services—needed to accommodate the new seeds.

Not only were industrial projects more appealing; politicians in the poor countries assumed that they could depend more or less permanently on food aid from abroad. Urged, early in 1965, to build food reserves in India as a hedge against possible crop failures, one Indian government official replied, "Why should we bother? Our reserves are the wheat fields of Kansas."

This attitude, typical of politicians in many poor countries, was changed by the inexorable pressure of population on available food supplies and land. It became obvious that even the vast resources of American agriculture could not meet indefinitely the widening food deficits, particularly in India and Pakistan.

Just prior to World War II, the countries of Asia, Africa, and Latin America were exporting grain, mostly to Western Europe, where it earned valuable foreign exchange. After World War II, all of these regions became net food importers, principally from the United States. By 1960, the net grain inflow had climbed to 19 million tons yearly; by 1966 it had reached 36 million tons. The population explosion had made the larger poor countries—mainland China, India, Pakistan, Indonesia, and Brazil—importers of food on a massive scale.

The adverse food-population trends came into sharp focus in 1966 and 1967, after the Indo-Pakistan subcontinent suffered two consecutive monsoon failures. The United States, the only country carrying food reserves of any size, responded by shipping one fifth of its wheat crop to India. Transportation of this huge quantity of grain required some 600 ships, the largest maritime assemblage since the Allied Forces crossed the English Channel on D-Day. For a period of two years, more than 60 million Indians were sustained entirely by American food shipments.

Had the United States been unable to respond, the result would have been famine for millions and possibly tens of millions, a human tragedy that would have rivaled World War II. This close brush with famine became a critical turning point in global efforts to combat hunger.

In the mid-'sixties, the United States government began to realize that the ready availability of food aid had helped to bring on the crisis. Economic planners and finance ministers in the poor countries, faced with unlimited needs and scarce resources, were continually tempted to cut corners in agriculture, knowing that any resulting food deficits could and would be filled by aid shipments from the United States. Thus, for example, a four-year aid agreement with India, signed in 1959, in which the United States agreed to supply 16 million tons of wheat and one million tons of rice, allowed the Indian government to postpone any meaningful decisions to improve agriculture.

By early 1965, it had become obvious that the United States would have to change its policy. The food aid provided under Public Law 480 as a means of relieving hunger while simultaneously disposing of unwanted American surpluses alleviated both problems but solved neither. In some countries it was actually aggravating the problem of hunger by depressing the prices of wheat and rice to the point where it was unprofitable for local farmers to use fertilizer.

In 1965, therefore, policy shifted from direct food aid toward helping poor countries to increase their own food production. Financial support for agricultural development abroad by the Agency for International Development (AID) jumped from $170 million in 1963 to nearly $600 million in 1967, most of it allotted to financing shipments of fertilizer. A further decision was made to mobilize the technical resources of the United States more effectively, particularly those of the Department of Agriculture and the land-grant universities. At the same time, the government began to allocate food aid in terms of months rather than years, as had been the practice. This "short tether" policy had a marked effect in the poor countries. In particular, it helped to bolster prices and, just as important, the anticipation of higher prices in the local grain markets.

The "short tether" policy became feasible because U.S. reserves of grain had been reduced to a desirable working level. This made it possible for the first time to strengthen the hands of those politicians in the poor countries who were pressing for more action to increase the local capacity to produce food. As the Agriculture Minister of one such country put it at the time, "Now I can get the Finance Minister to return my phone calls."

Although the policies of the United States played a vitally important part in creating the necessary political-economic climate for the new revolution, it was the strong personal backing of crop-production campaigns by such key leaders as Prime Minister Demirel of Turkey and Presidents Ayub of Pakistan and Marcos of the Philippines, combined with realistic economic policies and efficient management of government programs, that gave the agricultural revolution its impetus. Prime Minister Demirel personally directed the new wheat program in his country. Under President Ayub, fertilizer availability in Pakistan increased several fold during the 1960's. In the Philippines, President Marcos stressed three objectives during his administration—more rice, more roads, and better schools. His successful campaign for re-election in late 1969 was keyed to his success in bringing the Islands to self-sufficiency in rice.

India's Minister of Agriculture, C. S. Subramaniam, rose to the threat of famine by working, on the one hand, to organize a huge internal food-distribution effort and, on the other, to launch India's high-yielding-varieties program. Thus, he regained the initiative for India in the battle for survival and set the stage for the exciting gains in food-grain production made in 1968 and 1969.

In August, 1966, Afghanistan's Prime Minister Maiwandwal called a meeting of his cabinet and assessed each Ministry 2.5 per cent of its current operating budget. This assessment was used to launch an accelerated wheat-production program, an effort which eliminated Afghanistan's wheat imports, at least temporarily, in 1969.

The economic climate for agriculture during the 1966–68 period was extraordinarily favorable, probably more so than at any other time in recent history. The widespread failure of food production to keep pace with demand in individual countries, combined with a worldwide reduction in exportable surpluses, had caused grain prices to rise. The consecutive monsoon failures on the Indo-Pakistan subcontinent, which created a scarcity of foodstuffs, greatly enhanced the farmers' bargaining position in the marketplace. The world rice price, normally about $120 per ton, soared past $200 in 1967. Little rice was available to fill the deficit, and a billion low-income rice consumers were forced to tighten their belts. Government after government began to adopt guaranteed minimum prices for wheat and rice, intended to assure farmers that prices at harvest time would justify the use of fertilizer at planting time.

ENGINES OF CHANGE

The agricultural breakthrough has not yet been achieved in all poor countries, and it is so far confined to cereals, principally wheat and rice. But it has already arrested the deteriorating food situation in some of the most populous countries of Asia—India, Pakistan, Indonesia, Turkey, and the Philippines. The incidence of hunger is beginning to decline as food consumption rises.

Rapid increases in cereal production are but one aspect of the agricultural breakthrough. The new seeds are bringing far-reaching changes in every segment of society. They may be to the agricultural revolution in the poor countries what the steam engine was to the Industrial Revolution in Europe.

Most obviously, the new seeds demand an entirely different set of husbandry practices. If farmers are to realize the genetic potential of these seeds, they may need to increase the plant population or to change the time of planting or the depth of seeding; they must irrigate more frequently and with more precision; they must use fertilizer in large quantities and weed carefully lest the fertilizer be converted into weeds instead of grain.

As the mold of tradition is broken, farmers become more susceptible to change in other areas. They may become more interested in education and more receptive to family planning. The economic and political relationship between farmers and the rest of the economy begins to change fundamentally. Using purchased inputs, and marketing additional production, peasant farmers are drawn into the mainstream of modern economic life. At the same time, the industrial sector turns more and more to the countryside as a market, not only for farm supplies, but for consumer goods as well.

PROMISES AND PROBLEMS

Part I discusses the technical innovations which are revolutionizing life on the farm. The full impact of the breakthrough will be felt in the 'seventies. Continuing change is assured, in part because the transfer of technology across national boundaries is being institutionalized by research institutes, supported by the foundations, the multinational operations of agribusiness corporations, and national and international development agencies (see Part II).

Social change is a delicate and often dangerous process, not without its costs. The breakthrough in production is already spotlighting the serious inadequacies of food-marketing systems. The dramatic gains in income being realized by farmers who are able to use the new seeds abruptly widens the gap in living standards, and the consequent conflicts, between them and those who are still tied to traditional husbandry practices. The long list of "second generation" problems growing out of the success of the production breakthrough is discussed in Part III.

These second-generation problems cannot be solved by farmers alone. In the next decade, the problems of agricultural development in the poor countries will be much more political than technical, and solutions will depend much more on politicians than on farmers. In particular, the new seeds will directly affect the flow of people from the countryside to the cities. With enlightened policies on farm mechanization and land reform, the flow can be contained; if these policies are mismanaged, the cities may be choked with displaced rural populations. These possibilities are discussed in Part IV.

From the humanitarian point of view, the great promise of the agricultural revolution in the poor countries is the possibility of eliminating hunger and creating an environment in which population growth will be slowed and eventually stabilized. The new seeds are forcing a redefinition of the population problem. Attention is shifting from food supplies to jobs, for today it is not so much an inadequate food supply as unemployment and the uneven distribution of income that make hunger persist (Part V).

The impact of the agricultural revolution extends far beyond the borders of the poor countries in which it is taking place. The new seeds promise eventually to alter the global pattern of agriculture because they tend to redress the production advantage in favor of the tropical-subtropical regions. Thus the recent production increases have resulted in deep cutbacks in United States wheat acreage. A crisis in the world grain market is imminent because the food-production breakthroughs are occurring just as Europe and Japan are pursuing highly protectionist agricultural policies. The stage is now set for a major confrontation between the rich and poor countries over how to rationalize world agricultural trade. The pivotal question is whether the rich countries that do not have a comparative advantage in cereals are prepared to open their internal markets to cereal exports from the poor countries.

But the challenge to the rich countries posed by the new agricultural breakthroughs in the poor countries is even broader and deeper than this. As they have done in the past, science and technology have magnified both the problems and the opportunities facing the community of nations. The agricultural revolution suggests an agenda for the 'seventies (Part VI) that can give substance and hope to the idea of an interdependent world, a "global village." Man's hope for peace in this century rests upon the willingness of rich and poor nations alike to work on such an agenda.

I

The Technological
Breakthrough

2

The New Seeds

Until recently, virtually all of the major breakthroughs in agricultural technology originated in the temperate zones. Even though a great deal of research has been devoted to plantation agriculture in the tropics, the prime beneficiaries have been outsiders, those in the rich countries to whom the commodities are sold. Those in the tropics were at best residual beneficiaries, forced to make do with an agricultural technology developed in northwestern Europe, the United States, or Japan, a technology admirably adapted to the temperate climates but usually poorly suited to the tropics.

The new seeds were designed to capitalize on the unique natural advantages of tropical-subtropical areas, particularly the wealth of solar energy available only in such climates. On bright, sunny days, land close to the Equator receives 56 to 59 per cent of the potential radiant energy, as compared with only 47 per cent at 40 degrees latitude (Washington, D. C.). These new seeds are the product of the first systematic attempt to devise a technology to capitalize on this and to help improve the lot of hundreds of millions of people who live in material poverty.

THE ENGINEERING PROBLEM

Plant breeders are biological engineers. Just as Henry Ford designed the Model-T to meet the varied needs of middle-class America, so the plant breeders designed the new wheat and rice varieties to meet the varied needs of peasant farmers in the poor regions of the world. The real challenge to the designers of the new seeds was to develop cereal varieties that were not only responsive to fertilizer but also adaptable throughout the poor regions of the world. If the poor countries have the advantage of a great supply of solar energy, they have the disadvantage of great variation in soil conditions. Just as the Model-T had to be able to run on all kinds of roads in all kinds of weather, so the new seeds had to be able to grow under a wide variety of soil and climatic conditions.

In the tropics, traditional food varieties are the result of centuries of natural selection, undisturbed by any scientific attempt to control the plant's environment. Left to its own devices, nature chooses strains that will survive under prevailing growing conditions. These traditional strains have to fight for survival against weeds and in heavy rains and floods. This makes for a tall, thin-strawed plant that can keep its head above water when there is flooding and can compete successfully with weeds for its share of sunlight.

Introducing fertilizer into this natural environment is a complex task. Traditional strains are not responsive to fertilizer; when it is applied liberally, they become topheavy with grain and fall over, or "lodge," before the grain is ripe. Their tall straw, so necessary for survival in nature's environment, is too weak to carry the added load of grain generated by the application of fertilizer.

This problem was overcome first in Japan and then in the United States. The Japanese isolated a dwarfing gene which produced a sturdy, short-strawed wheat capable of carrying a heavy head of grain. The new dwarf wheats owe their existence to this technological breakthrough. However, mass application came to the poor countries in a roundabout way.

The dwarfing gene was brought to the United States in 1947 by Dr. S. C. Salmon of the United States Department of Agriculture. The Japanese variety did not travel well, however. It was only when another USDA scientist, Dr. Orville Vogel, incorporated the Japanese dwarf gene into his own local breeding materials that a successful dwarf variety was developed. The resulting variety, called Gaines wheat, produced world-record yields in the irrigated and high-rainfall growing conditions of the Pacific Northwest.

Meanwhile, Dr. Norman Borlaug, Director of the Rockefeller Foundation's wheat-breeding program in Mexico, heard about Dr. Vogel's work and obtained some of Dr. Vogel's breeding materials containing the dwarfing gene. He refined Gaines wheat to make it more suitable for use in Mexico. In the process, he achieved a second major breakthrough in plant breeding.

Dr. Borlaug wanted to develop a dwarf wheat that would perform well under the varied growing conditions of Mexico. He amassed germ plasm from Japan, the United States, Australia, and Colombia and then began growing two alternate crops of wheat each year at two different sites, a summer crop just south of the United States border, and another crop in winter near Mexico City, some eight hundred miles away. The two sites differed in day length, or photoperiod, as well as in many other environmental factors. Given the cosmopolitan ancestry of his seeds, Dr. Borlaug was able to produce a dwarf wheat variety that was remarkably adapted to a range of growing conditions. The Mexican dwarf wheats today are growing successfully in latitudes near the Equator, where days are of uniform length and also in higher latitudes, such as Turkey, where day length varies greatly by season. This adaptability was something new. Hitherto, the dwarf wheats had performed well only under conditions comparable to those in which they were first bred.

FROM WHEAT TO RICE

Buoyed by the success of the Mexican wheats, and keenly aware that most of the world's poor eat rice, the Rockefeller and Ford Foundations joined forces in 1962 to establish the International Rice Research Institute on land provided by the Philippine government at Los Banos, near Manila. A crack team of scientists was assembled from the United States, the Philippines, Taiwan, and elsewhere under the direction of Dr. Robert Chandler, formerly President of the University of New Hampshire. The objective was to produce a cosmopolitan dwarf rice strain comparable to the Mexican wheats.

The team assembled some ten thousand strains of rice from every corner of the world and began a patient process of crossbreeding. Success came early when a tall, vigorous variety from Indonesia, called Peta, was combined with a dwarf rice from Taiwan, called Deo-geo-woo-gen, to produce the "miracle rice," IR-8. When properly managed, IR-8 has proved easily capable of doubling the yield of most local rices in Asia.

IR-8 and an increasingly popular new strain, IR-5, have already proved responsive to fertilizer in a wide range of growing conditions in several countries. IR-8 and its cousins can effectively absorb up to 120 pounds of fertilizer per acre without lodging, while traditional varieties usually lodge after the application of 40 pounds.

Not only do the new varieties respond to much heavier dosages of fertilizer, they are far more efficient in its use. One pound of nitrogen applied to the old varieties would yield close to 10 additional pounds of grain. David Hopper, a Rockefeller Foundation economist in New Delhi, calculates that a pound of nitrogen applied to the new seeds can yield up to 20 pounds of grain.[1]

In addition to being highly adaptable, the new rices are early maturing. IR-8 matures in 120 days, as compared with 150–180 days for traditional varieties. As will be seen in the next chapter, this shorter growth cycle often means an extra crop, if not of rice, of something else. It means that the new

[1] W. David Hopper, *Strategy for the Conquest of Hunger*, New York: Rockefeller Foundation, April, 1968, p. 107.

seeds are not only more efficient users of sunlight but of land itself.

A WINDFALL GAIN

The new seeds have been supplied to the poor countries on a virtually costless basis; millions of farmers who are planting them are reaping huge windfall gains in production. Countries such as India, Pakistan, and Turkey imported samples of Mexican wheats for testing. Once the seeds' adaptability to local conditions was established, these countries imported them from Mexico by the shipload (see Table 1) , and at prices only marginally higher than world market prices for wheat. Since these countries were already importing wheat, the real additional cost was only the modest difference between the cost of the Mexican wheat seed and the world market price.

TABLE 1

Imports of High-Yielding Mexican Wheat Seed into Asia

Country	Crop Year	Tonnage Imported
Afghanistan	1967	170
India	1965	250
	1966	18,000
Nepal	1966	38
	1967	450
Pakistan	1965	350
	1966	50
	1967	42,000
Turkey	1967	60
	1968	22,000

SOURCE: Dana Dalrymple, *Imports and Plantings of High-Yielding Varieties of Wheat and Rice in the Less Developed Nations*, Washington, D.C.: International Agricultural Development Service, U.S. Department of Agriculture, 1968, mimeo, pp. 2–3.

Not only was the new technology essentially free but, because the seeds could be imported in bulk, the time required for seed multiplication was greatly reduced. Normally the

development of a new variety begins with a small handful of
seed which is multiplied to a half bushel, then a quarter ton,
ten tons, four hundred tons, eventually producing enough to
release the seed commercially. Pakistan imported 42,000 tons
of the new wheat seeds in 1967–68, enough to plant more than
a million acres. When this crop was harvested, it provided
enough seed to cover all of Pakistan's wheat land, thus tele-
scoping into two years a process normally requiring several
years.

Imports of seed rice from the Philippines similarly accelerated the diffusion of the high-yielding dwarf rices, such as
IR-8. Since a ton of rice plants several times as much land as
a ton of wheat, the imported tonnages are far lower for rice
than for wheat.

Perhaps more important than the actual tonnage of the
dwarf wheats and rices imported is the prototype they represent, which local plant breeders can refine and modify specifically for local growing conditions. The new seeds are thus
raising the sights of agricultural scientists, ushering in a
renaissance in agricultural research. Two promising rices, released in Eastern India during 1969, are Jaya and Padma, both
local modifications of the dwarf prototype. Other local modifications are being released in Ceylon, Malaysia, and Thailand. Local improvements on the dwarf wheat prototypes are
already in widespread use in India and Pakistan. As plant-
breeding efforts continue, the first generation of high-yielding
varieties will be replaced with a second generation. In some
countries this process is already under way.

It is, of course, not the scientists and technologists who are
responsible for the vast and rapid acceptance of the new seeds
but the millions of farmers, particularly in Asia, who decided to plant them and in so doing found their incomes increasing two-, three-, and even fourfold. The area planted to
high-yielding cereals in Asia in the 1964–65 crop year was
estimated at 200 acres, and that largely for experimental and

trial purposes. By 1968–69, 34 million acres were covered.
The expansion progressed as follows:

1964–65	200 acres
1965–66	37,000 acres
1966–67	4,800,000 acres
1967–68	20,000,000 acres
1968–69	34,000,000 acres

This acreage consists largely of Mexican wheats and IRRI
rices, but it also includes locally developed high-yielding rices,
such as ADT-27 in India and H-4 in Ceylon, as well as limited
plantings of high-yielding corn and sorghum. Because they
proved so profitable to farmers, adoption of the new varieties
spread far more rapidly than was anticipated, raising cereal
production at an unexpected rate. If it is assumed that replacement of local varieties with high-yielding seeds raised
output by a half-ton per acre—a conservative assumption—
the 34 million acres planted in 1968–69 expanded the Asian
food supply by 17 million tons, roughly the equivalent of two
billion dollars' worth of grain!

PLANT BREEDERS' AGENDA

Table 2 shows how the new seeds have spread in selected
countries. At present, less than one seventh of the wheat and
rice land in Asia, excluding Mainland China, is planted to the
new seeds. Because this land is relatively well irrigated and
fertile, it produces a disproportionately large share of the
region's food. In Africa and Latin America the new seeds are
not being used so widely as in Asia, but they are being successfully introduced in some countries, and a considerable
amount of experimentation is taking place in others. Introduction of the Mexican wheats into Morocco and Tunisia,
though more recent than in Asia, is proceeding successfully.
Acreage is expected to expand rapidly in the early 'seventies.

TABLE 2
Area Planted to High-Yielding Mexican Wheats

Country	Crop Year	Planted Area (acres)
Afghanistan	1967	4,500
	1968	65,000
	1969	300,000
India	1966	7,400
	1967	1,278,000
	1968	6,681,000
	1969	10,000,000
Nepal	1966	3,500
	1967	16,200
	1968	61,300
Pakistan	1966	12,000
	1967	255,000
	1968	1,800,000
	1969	6,000,000
Turkey	1968	420,000
	1969	1,780,000

SOURCE: Dalrymple, *op. cit.*, p. 2.

The process of replacing traditional varieties of grain with high-yielding ones in Asia will continue for the foreseeable future, but probably not at the pace of the past few years. Although they are adapted to a wide range of growing conditions, the Mexican wheats have a pronounced yield advantage over local wheats only when they are grown under irrigated or high-rainfall conditions. Under dryland farming conditions, where little or no fertilizer can be used, they offer little if any advantage. The dwarf rices, conversely, perform poorly and sometimes fail completely in conditions of natural flooding or in rainfed fields where they may be submerged for some time. Expansion of the area planted to high-yielding wheats is already slowing somewhat in both India and Pakistan, for example, as the additional land with suitable water supply diminishes. But there is likely to be considerable expansion into countries that are not yet using the new seeds; Iran and Iraq, for example, have just begun to plant the new wheats. But in the parts of the continent where the high-yielding varieties are well established, water supply and water control will act as the principal constraints to further spread. (Other constraints are discussed in subsequent chapters.)

The biological engineers are at work on these problems, developing wheats that will raise yields under low rainfall conditions and rices that are more tolerant of flooding. At the same time, both farmers and governments are steadily expanding and intensifying irrigation and flood-control systems. Only a minor part of the cereal-producing land in Asia can be planted profitably with the seeds that exist now, but still more effective seeds are constantly being developed.

Farmers in the poor countries increasingly view the future in terms of new seeds, new techniques, and a more productive life. Symbolizing this attitude is the response of the Filipino Farmer of the Year, 58-year-old Andres de la Cruz, when asked what variety of rice he was going to plant next season. "I don't know," he unhesitatingly answered. "I'm still waiting for a newer variety."

3

New Irrigation Strategies

The new seeds are generating an enormous thirst for irrigation water among millions of farmers in the poor countries where they are being introduced. For many, water has suddenly become the key to a better life. With an adequate supply of water, farmers can use the new wheats or rices, raise their living standards, and enter the twentieth century; without it, they remain tied to traditional agriculture, merely eking out a subsistence living.

The new seeds and associated technologies are abruptly altering the economics of both water use and water-resource development. They produce more grain per unit of water since the increase in yields usually surpasses the increase in water use. The fact that the dwarf rices mature in four months rather than the five or six required for traditional varieties reduces the irrigation period. Now that water has become the pivotal factor determining whether the new seeds can be used, its value is climbing sharply.

Already the new seeds, and exceptionally favorable farm prices, are having an effect on irrigation strategies. Tubewells (closed cylindrical shafts driven into the ground) and electric pumps have suddenly become popular with farmers. Accordingly, governments have put more emphasis on encouraging small-scale irrigation that farmers can install in a matter of days or weeks rather than on huge irrigation systems that take many years and millions of dollars to construct.

Traditional irrigation systems in such countries as India and Pakistan, originally planned and built by British engineers at a much earlier stage of agricultural technology, were designed primarily as a defense against drought. Their purpose was to prevent crop failure, not to maximize crop yields. A small amount of water was spread thinly over a large land area.

But the new seeds, responsive as they are to heavy applications of fertilizer, demand a more intensive use of water. The new rice varieties in particular are more productive in the dry seasons, when there is more sunlight, assuming of course that an adequate supply of water is available. Modern irrigation systems designed to optimize yields, such as those in Japan and California, will deliver five times as much water to a given area of land as traditional systems, such as the one in West Pakistan.

In India and Pakistan, the greater use of water has meant a dramatic increase in small-scale irrigation, particularly tubewells. Pakistani farmers installed 32,000 private tubewells, costing from $1,000 to $2,500 apiece, over a five-year span during the midsixties. The installation of each 5,000 tubewells in West Pakistan adds an estimated one million acre-feet to the yearly supply of irrigation water. Most important, this new source is under the farmer's personal management, enabling him to control very precisely the amount and timing of the water delivered to his crops.

During the 1968 crop year, Indian farmers installed 42,000 tubewells, which should provide an additional eight million acre-feet of water. The Indian government installed another thousand to be operated by the state. Farmers purchased 200,000 pump sets, a large proportion of which replaced traditional bullock- or hand-powered water-lifting devices. India's farmers invested $100 million in wells and pumps in crop year 1968, a vast increase over a few years earlier.

This dramatic turn toward tubewells as a source of irrigation water—made possible by the work of AID technologists in the 1950's—was the result of many factors in addition to the introduction of the new seeds. The two successive monsoon failures in the Indian subcontinent underlined the risks of overdependence on the monsoon and surface-water supplies. Even in good monsoon years, the rainfall is concentrated in a few months of the year. To make water available in the dry season, when the yield potential of the new seeds, particularly rice, is so much higher because of the greater availability of solar energy, and when so many of the resources of traditional farms are underutilized, it is necessary either to impound and conserve the monsoon rains or to augment the water supply by other means. Tapping underground water resources, which are independent of seasonal variations in the monsoon, is one obvious way both to augment the water supply and to minimize the risks of a monsoon failure.

TVA's in the LDC's

Farmers in the less-developed countries, such as India and Pakistan, have also turned to tubewells because large irrigation works, often the byproducts of multipurpose hydroelectric dams, have sometimes proved inefficient. The multipurpose dam, so fascinating to engineers, has its purposes in the poor countries, but it has yet to live up to the dreams of its promoters. Such projects tie up large blocks of capital for long periods of time. Seventy-two major irrigation projects undertaken in India between 1951 and 1965 cover a total command area of 13.4 million hectares, but only one fourth of this area was being irrigated by 1966. And the story is much the same in other countries.

The huge expenditures required for these undertakings are often justified on the ground that they bring other benefits, particularly new supplies of electric power; the World Bank, which has financed many such projects, tends to justify its investments in multipurpose dams solely in terms of power benefits. It is certainly easier to use power than irrigation water as the measure of the worth of an investment; the delivery of water to farmers at the right time is a much more complex task than the delivery of power to a factory or community facility.

But the effective delivery of irrigation waters from a large centralized system to masses of peasant farmers requires a degree of communication between the farmer and the administering agency that is still far beyond the ability of most poor countries. Peasant farmers in traditional societies are by and large unwilling to pay for water delivered by "the government," even where the government provides the means of getting the water to the farmers. There is little confidence in the reliability of government services. On the other hand, when a peasant farmer realizes that he can recover his own investment in a tubewell in as little as two years and at the same time get irrigation waters subject to his immediate control, he will act. The new seeds have brought this opportunity to thousands of farmers in a brief period, as is demonstrated by the investment of $50 million in 32,000 private tubewells by "peasant farmers" of West Pakistan!

The electrification of rural communities is facilitating the rapid spread of small irrigation. The cost of irrigation waters for farmers who are able to use electric engines is usually about a third less than for those in similar circumstances who have to rely on diesel engines. But once farmers served by electricity invest in pumps and engines, those in neighboring areas without access to electricity tend to invest in tubewells and pumps powered by diesels.

Throughout most of Asia today, finance ministers are beginning to encourage small-scale irrigation financed largely by individual farmers simply to reduce pressures on the government's budget. The government of Pakistan has lifted all import restrictions on low-lift pumps for use in East Pakistán.

In India rural areas with underground water reserves are being given priority in electrification over residential areas and rural areas lacking such reserves.

Farmers in the delta areas of Thailand, South Vietnam, and East Pakistan are investing heavily in pumps to lift water from low-flowing streams and canals to field levels during the dry season. The combination of high-yielding rices and favorable prices makes such investment among the most profitable a farmer can undertake. It means that fields once idle during the dry season are now green with a second crop of rice.

In East Pakistan it is proving less costly to expand production of the new rice varieties by using wells and pumps during the dry season than through the massive investments in flood control required to create conditions suitable for their use during the wet season. Of 22 million cultivated acres in East Pakistan, it is estimated that five million acres can be irrigated for dry-season cultivation by using small pumps to lift water from the low-flowing canals and rivers such as the Brahmaputra, the Ganges, and their tributaries.[1]

Four fifths of the world's irrigated land is located in Asia, the Middle East, and North Africa—regions containing at least three fourths of those families in the world with incomes below $100 a year. But the distribution of irrigated land is very uneven and the total acreage inadequate. In Asia, where nine tenths of the world's rice crop is produced, only a third of the rice land is irrigated. Most of the remainder is rainfed, either by flooding or by trapping monsoon rainfall in fields surrounded by low earthen dikes, called "bunds." In Thailand and India, only one fifth and one third, respectively, of the rice crops is irrigated, but in Taiwan and Japan, where highly sophisticated irrigation systems have been developed,

---

[1] Ghulum Mohammad, "Development of Irrigated Agriculture in East Pakistan: Some Basic Considerations," *The Pakistan Development Review*, Autumn, 1966, p. 363.

nearly all the rice crop is irrigated. Thus, much of the potential for irrigation in Asia has yet to be realized.

As population presses more and more on the available supply of water in the poor countries, the efficiency of water use will ultimately determine to a large degree the food supply per person. Increasingly, the lack of water rather than of land is limiting food production. We must therefore begin to concern ourselves more with man:water ratios and less with man:land ratios.

The new seeds and the new approaches to irrigation that they stimulate offer great hope for countries whose populations are growing fastest and exerting the greatest demands on the food supply. The greater yield potential of the new seeds is generating pressure to improve the timing and delivery of water to farmers from the large irrigation structures such as those in the Indus Basin system, on the Zambesi at Kariba, or on the Nile at Aswan. The greater financial returns offered by the new seeds must now be taken into account in developing water resources in East Pakistan, the Mekong system, and other as-yet-undeveloped river systems. These factors and the impetus the new seeds are giving farmers to invest in their own sources of irrigation water are but another measure of the potential of the agricultural revolution.

4

Farming Around the Calendar

Wherever grain is grown, nature and tradition have usually combined to set a limit of one crop a year. In the higher latitudes, low temperatures during the winter preclude a second cereal crop. In the tropics, the lack of water during the dry season and the inability to maintain soil fertility have traditionally limited multiple cropping. Low temperatures remain an insurmountable obstacle in the temperate zones, but the constraints in the tropics are being removed by the new technologies.

Farming around the calendar with two, three, and occasionally even four crops per year is becoming feasible in the tropical and subtropical regions. Scientists at Los Banos regularly harvest three crops of rice per year. Each acre they plant yields six tons annually, roughly three times the average annual yield of corn, the highest yielding cereal in the United States. Farmers in the State of Mysore, India, are now producing three crops of hybrid corn every 14 months, using intensive applications of both fertilizer and irrigation water.

As multiple cropping spreads, it is profoundly altering the way of life in the countryside, divorcing it from the traditional seasonal crop cycle, which dictated not only planting and harvesting times but the timing of religious festivals, weddings, and a host of other social events as well. Land which traditionally lay idle during the dry season is being used more and more to produce food.

DISCOVERING THE DRY SEASON

With the new agricultural technologies, farmers in the tropics are beginning to discover the potential for expanding food production in the dry, sunny season. Data from both Indonesia and the Philippines show higher yields in the dry season than in the wet season for five high-yielding varieties grown at several different sites. Although environmental conditions varied widely among the sites, dry-season yields were consistently higher, averaging 52 per cent above those during the wet season (Table 3).

TABLE 3

Yields from High-Yielding Rice Varieties in Wet and Dry Seasons
(Pounds Milled Rice per acre) *

Variety	Site	Wet Season (pounds)	Dry Season (pounds)	Excess of Dry Season Over Wet (per cent)
Syntha	Indonesia	2,749	3,407	24
Syntha	Central Java	2,869	3,885	35
IR-8	Philippines-Maligaya	3,775	4,172	11
IR-8	Philippines-IRRI	3,054	5,497	80
IR-8	Philippines	1,896	4,232	23
BPI-76-1	Philippines-IRRI	2,150	3,789	76
BPI-76-1	Philippines-IRRI	2,308	3,884	68
Taichung N. 1	Philippines-IRRI	2,464	3,514	43
IR-9-60	Philippines-IRRI	2,799	4,073	46
	Average	2,673	4,050	52

* Yield data, from the International Rice Research Institute and the Asian Development Bank, were often the byproduct of research plots designed to test other variables, such as fertilizer application. Nonetheless, they do indicate the contrast in performance between the wet and dry seasons.

Much rice land in the tropics lacks the necessary water to produce a second crop of rice during the dry season but can produce other crops with lower water requirements. In some circumstances, for example, a crop of wheat can be produced with only a third the water needed for rice. Among the cereals, sorghum is perhaps most in harmony with nature as regards water. Sorghum responds well to intensive irrigation, but at the same time it tolerates drought far better than rice, corn, or even wheat. It becomes dormant in the event of severe drought, resuming growth when moisture supplies are replenished.

In central and northern India, and in parts of Pakistan where rice is normally grown during the rainy season, it is now possible to harvest the early-maturing rice in time to plant a crop of high-yielding wheat in the dry season. Grain sorghum is a natural to combine with rice in the dry season. With water and fertilizer, certain varieties of sorghum "tiller" after harvest—i.e., generate new stems and leaves to produce a second and third crop of grain from the original planting. Scientists at Los Banos are harvesting eight tons of grain a year from a single acre planted successively with rice and sorghum. Heretofore, farmers in some parts of Asia have harvested scarcely half a ton per year.

The economic advantages of farming during the dry season are obvious. Increased utilization of farm labor, draft animals, and farm equipment which formerly lay idle in the dry season, combined with higher yields, makes dry-season cropping exceedingly profitable. The likelihood of substantially higher profits justifies investments in dry-season irrigation facilities, such as tubewells, or water-impounding structures, which may not be financially attractive with the older varieties.

THE POTENTIAL FOR MULTIPLE CROPPING

In countries where holdings are small and possibilities for enlarging them are nonexistent, more intensive use of land through multiple cropping may be the only avenue to a better life. More intensive cropping is in many ways ideal for small family farms, where labor is abundant and relatively inexpensive. Replacing a single crop of a traditional variety with two high-yielding crops broadens a farmer's economic base since it enables him both to expand his food supply and to create a store of feed grain for a small livestock enterprise.

The genetic characteristics of the new varieties—high yields, early maturity, and reduced sensitivity to photoperiod—open new vistas for double cropping. The higher yield potential of the new seeds in itself provides a strong incentive for multiple cropping.

Early maturation, which sometimes reduces the growing season by a third, makes many new cropping combinations possible. Their reduced sensitivity to day length permits many of the new varieties to be planted throughout the year in the tropical-subtropical regions, in sharp contrast with traditional seeds, whose biological clocks are keyed to a specific seasonal day-length cycle.

The science of multiple cropping is still in its infancy. The potential has scarcely been exploited; nor have the problems it generates been clearly identified. Producing two or more crops a year is not an unmixed blessing; it sometimes creates deficiencies in minor soil nutrients and special pest and disease problems. There may be special problems of water management, and in some cases there is the problem of harvesting and drying grain while the monsoon is in full sway.

Nevertheless, the potential benefits are arousing the interest of farmers and governments alike. Plans to reach self-sufficiency in rice in Malaysia, Ceylon, and India rest heavily on expansion of the double-cropped area. Large-scale irrigation projects financed by the World Bank, such as the Mahweli project in Ceylon and the Muda project in Malaysia, are designed to expand rice double-cropping.

The Indian Agricultural Research Institute, with field stations located throughout India, is experimenting with various multiple-cropping combinations. One four-crop rotation includes rice during the wet season, a short-season vegetable crop, wheat during the winter season and an oilseed crop in the spring. India, which planted 15 million acres to short-season cereals during the 1968–69 dry season, plans a steady expansion in the years ahead. Tanjore District, one of India's well-irrigated rice-producing districts, is currently double cropping one fourth of its rice land and plans to harvest two rice crops a year on all its rice land beginning in the early 'seventies.

Nine per cent of Pakistan's crop land produced two crops in 1947. By 1965 the figure had risen to only 13 per cent. Since then, however, the percentage of double-cropped land has increased rapidly as the new seeds spread. Farmers in southern Brazil are beginning to double-crop winter wheat with summer soybeans. Double cropping has helped Mexico to achieve a fivefold increase in sorghum production over the past five years.

The potential for multiple cropping is suggested by the diligence of the Taiwanese farmers, who expanded the multiple-cropped area from 18 per cent of the total crop land in 1946 to 89 per cent in 1966. By 1969 Taiwanese farmers were harvesting an average of two crops on all their crop land. With its intensive cropping, Taiwan is an exporter of rice; limited to single cropping, it would be heavily dependent on imports.

ALTERING THE SEASONAL RHYTHM

Historically tied to the monsoon or rainy season, agriculture in the tropics and subtropics is developing a new rhythm. Farmers may be seen harvesting and planting in adjacent fields, with crops in the field representing all stages of growth and maturity. The farmers of Mysore, India, growing three crops of corn every 14 months, are finding that their planting dates change from one year to the next.

Now that chemical fertilizer is becoming available, farmers no longer must rely on the slow, gradual intraseasonal recharge of nutrients. Fertilizer applications can be geared to meet the nutritional requirements of continuous cropping.

For society as a whole in the poor countries, multiple cropping means a smoother flow of commodities into the marketplace as the harvest is spread evenly throughout the year. Gains in farm production through more intensive cropping systems help to expand exports or to reduce imports, thus increasing the national income and conserving scarce foreign exchange. In this way, among others, the new rhythm in the countryside promises to affect the rhythm of the whole national economy.

Multiple cropping in the equatorial latitudes makes a virtue of the very solar energy that has such a debilitating effect on human beings in these regions. Fortunately, its potential is greatest where hunger and malnutrition are most acute—the tropical-subtropical regions, which are well endowed with solar energy and rainfall and have temperatures favorable to year-round crop growth.

5

The Yield Takeoff

Does the agricultural revolution really have a future? Or is it just an event, a kind of technological Camelot that will be remembered only for what might have been, rather than for what actually happened?

To the analyst there are two reasons for optimism. First, there has been a "yield takeoff"—that is, an abrupt transition from a condition of near-static yields to one of rapid, continuing increases. Secondly, this yield takeoff has already proved immensely profitable to millions of individual farmers. There is therefore a strong incentive for others to adopt the new technologies.

Of course, the process could conceivably be reversed by a great catastrophe, such as a third world war or disintegration of the political system in a major country such as India. But knowledge, like energy, once created is not easily destroyed. And the new agricultural technologies have now reached so many millions that profound change must be considered inevitable.

THE YIELD TAKEOFF

Progress, whether technological or economic, does not occur in a steady, even fashion but in fits and starts. This makes it logical to talk about technological or economic

36

breakthroughs or "takeoffs." Thus the new seeds have made possible a quantum jump in the production that farmers can get from an acre of land.

The yield takeoff in wheat, shown for three countries in Figure 1, is easiest to illustrate. The line for Mexico is most dramatic, reflecting not only the adoption of the dwarf wheats and the growing use of fertilizer by all wheat growers but also the fact that a very large share of the wheat crop was brought under irrigation in Mexico between 1950 and 1960. The

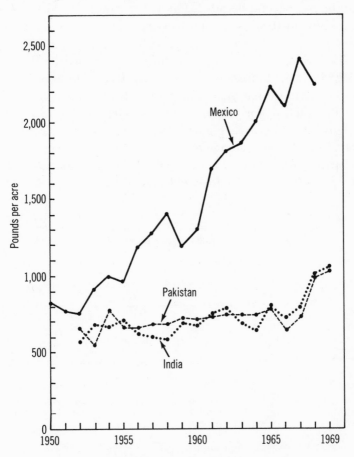

Figure 1. WHEAT YIELDS IN MEXICO, PAKISTAN, AND INDIA

combination of these factors produced a yield takeoff; in 15 years wheat yields have nearly tripled!

The wheat-growing areas in India and Pakistan are adjacent to one another and are influenced by the same weather cycles, so it is not surprising that the yield trends in two countries are quite similar. More important, they are similar to what happened in Mexico after the dwarf wheats began to spread there. Yield increases in these countries in the few years since the introduction of the new wheats exceed those of the past several decades. The recent annual yield increases in wheat in these two countries are more than double those following the introduction of hybrid corn in the United States. Several other poor countries—particularly Turkey, Afghanistan, Tunisia, Morocco, and Iran—appear to be on the verge of similar yield takeoffs in wheat.

The picture for rice is not yet so clear as for wheat (see Figure 2). The area planted to the new rices represents a much smaller percentage of the total crop area than the area planted to the new wheats. Nevertheless, Ceylon and West Pakistan have achieved a yield takeoff, and the Philippines,

TABLE 4

Wheat and Rice Production Trends in Selected Countries
(1,000 metric tons)

	Wheat		Rice		
Year	India	Pakistan	Ceylon	West Pakistan	Philippines
1960	10,322	3,938	611	1,547	2,408
1961	10,997	3,847	613	1,692	2,542
1962	12,072	4,129	682	1,645	2,579
1963	10,829	4,215	698	1,790	2,498
1964	9,853	4,197	716	2,028	2,595
1965	12,290	4,626	515	1,977	2,647
1966	10,424	3,786	649	2,049	2,657
1967	11,393	4,394	780	2,288	2,832,
1968	16,568	6,477	913	3,150	2,990
1969	18,000	7,000	na	na	na

SOURCE: U.S. Dept. of Agriculture.

Burma, Thailand, Indonesia, India, and East Pakistan are not far behind. Ceylon and West Pakistan, where virtually all rice land is irrigated, are advancing most rapidly. The Philippines, with four consecutive record rice harvests, has expanded rice production 17 per cent. This rise, although not spectacular, is enough to end a half-century of dependence on rice imports (see Table 4). Yield increases in the Philippines would have been more rapid if more of the rice land had been irrigated.

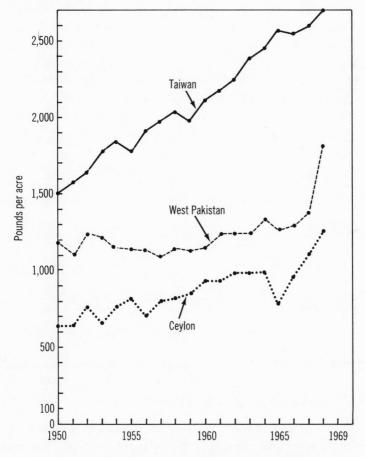

Figure 2. RICE YIELDS IN WEST PAKISTAN, CEYLON, AND TAIWAN

These yield takeoffs are occurring in the poor countries today at a much earlier stage in their development than the comparable breakthroughs that took place in North America and in Western Europe (see Table 5). In several of the Asian countries where the new seeds are being planted, only 25 per cent or less of the rural population is literate and per capita incomes average less than $100 a year. Both of these conventional indicators of "development" were significantly higher in the rich countries when their yield takeoffs occurred.

This fact does not mean that the agricultural revolution will unfold in the poor countries just as it did in the rich countries. It *does* mean that there is a real possibility that the poor countries can telescope into a few years much of the progress that it has taken decades to achieve elsewhere. This promise, so familiar to readers of the literature of develop-

TABLE 5
Dates of Yield Takeoffs in Selected Countries

Country	Crop	Year
Japan	Rice	1900
Taiwan	Rice	1915
United States	Corn	1940
Mexico	Wheat	1953
Philippines	Rice	1965
Pakistan	Wheat	1967
India	Wheat	1967
Ceylon	Rice	1967
Afghanistan	Wheat	1969
India	Rice	(1969)*
Turkey	Wheat	(1969)
Indonesia	Rice	(1970)
Iran	Wheat	(1970)
Morocco	Wheat	(1970)

* Parentheses indicate estimated date.

ment, has often bred more disillusionment than hope among peoples beset with the problems of mere survival. But the agricultural revolution gives substance to the promise as nothing else has in the poor countries up to now: farmers in these societies who are planting the new seeds are achieving in a matter of years progress that took decades in other countries.

Available data reflect yield changes for only single crops. The multiple cropping associated with the new seeds will raise land productivity further. Perhaps the most spectacular gains on record are those for Taiwan, where land productivity climbed 300 per cent between 1950 and 1965 as farmers both adopted improved rices and planted more crops per acre.

HIGHER INCOMES

What takes the notion of yield takeoff out of the realm of the abstract is the fact that the new seeds are abruptly raising incomes and living standards for literally millions of rural families in poor countries throughout the world.

Making generalizations about farmers' net incomes is hazardous since they depend mainly on price relationships of fertilizer and grain, both of which are continuously fluctuating. But the increases in net income where the new varieties have been planted are already of such magnitude as to be a central fact of the agricultural revolution. It is the incredible opportunity to raise incomes with the new seeds that underlies their rapid spread from country to country and from farm to farm.

Table 6 compares typical returns realized from the new varieties with those from local varieties. In Turkey, the net profits of farmers growing the dwarf wheats are two and a half times those derived from local varieties; in Pakistan, somewhat more than four to one; in India four and a half to one. In West Pakistan, with virtually all rice under irrigation, the margin in rice is just under two to one; in East Pakistan, where irrigation is limited and production of the high-yield-

TABLE 6
*Comparison of Net Income Per Acre for Local
and High-Yielding Varieties* *

	Local Varieties	High-Yielding Varieties
Wheat		
Turkey	$32	$ 80
Pakistan	$13	$ 54
India	$17	$ 76
Rice		
West Pakistan	$25	$ 45
East Pakistan	$30	$119
Philippines	$81	$140

* Data are drawn from a number of sources and represent either attempts to estimate national averages or the results of surveys. The data therefore should be taken as indicating the orders of magnitude of net income with the prices prevailing at the time of the estimate. Within any country there is a great variation, depending upon yields and costs of inputs. Most data are for the 1968 crop year.

ing rices is confined largely to the dry season, it is nearly four to one. In the Philippines the margin is much less; consumer resistance to the taste and texture of IR-8 reduced its price to 30 per cent below that of traditional varieties, thus offsetting some of its enormous yield advantage. Even so, incomes of farmers growing IR-8 were nearly twice those of farmers growing local varieties.

These are increases in net income, not gross income. As we have seen, the new seeds alone do not ensure high yield; they must be used with an adequate supply of water and plant nutrients. Farmers planting the new seeds therefore have to spend far more for production requisites. A Pakistani farmer spends five times more on fertilizer with the new seeds than with the traditional varieties. Filipino farmers planting IR-8 use four times as much fertilizer as with local varieties of rice. Yet net incomes still rose dramatically. In areas where the new seeds make multiple cropping possible, the rise in income will be even more pronounced.

These higher income figures do not mean that all farmers in the poor countries are going to become wealthy. They very probably do mean that social turmoil and discontent in the poor countries will be a central feature of the agricultural revolution, as is discussed in Chapter 9. The attraction of higher incomes promises to become a strong force for social change in those communities where the new seeds are being planted. Traditional agriculture is being rapidly commercialized, and for all intents and purposes this is an irreversible process.

The new seeds with their more efficient use of resources are reducing the costs of agricultural development and hence the costs of meeting food needs. New sources of savings and investment are being created. To what extent and in what form they will be transferred to the non-farm sector remains to be seen. They should help to finance industrial development through the investment of potentially greater rural savings in the non-farm sector, through the potentially higher tax take from the rural population, assuming that it can be collected, and through lower food costs to the urban population.

All that is certain now is that the new technologies make a significant reduction in the cost of agricultural development possible. As succeeding chapters will show, there are some formidable forces at work tending to make a reality out of that possibility, and others tending to frustrate it.

II

Transferring Technology

6

The Research Dividend

The transfer of the new seeds and associated technologies across national boundaries which has made the agricultural revolution possible is impressive in scale. But perhaps even more impressive is the fact that this transfer of technology is being institutionalized. This provides strong reason for believing that the momentum of the revolution will be sustained and will not dissipate after a few spectacular harvests, that it is not a one-shot affair but the beginning of a new era of continuous technological change and progress.

The institutions involved in this transfer include agricultural research centers (supported largely by private foundations), multinational corporations engaged in what has come to be called "agribusiness," national and international assistance agencies, and universities. American experience, as we shall see, has played a formative part in the roles each of these institutions has assumed.

THE PAYOFF ON RESEARCH

The conduct and dissemination of agricultural research is becoming institutionalized on a global scale simply because it has proved to be one of the most profitable investments mankind can make. Conversely, returns on investment in this activity are rising precisely because the results are being applied over an ever-wider geographical area.

For example, the initial investment made by the Rockefeller Foundation in wheat research in Mexico in 1943 has already yielded returns of 700 per cent *per year* for Mexico alone. The ultimate *global* return will not be known for many years, but it is apparent that it will be fantastically high. The acreage planted to Mexican wheats in Asia is now seven times that planted in Mexico!

Public and private investment in research on hybrid corn in the United States totaled $131 million as of 1955. At that time, the estimated return was seven dollars for every dollar invested. A more current estimate would probably show an even higher rate of return, since corn yields in the United States have nearly doubled since 1955. And this does not, of course, include the benefits from the use of these hybrids outside the United States. Wherever pertinent data are available, they indicate a good rate of return on investment in agricultural research. Table 7, for example, shows the returns realized on a selected range of research investments in the United States and Mexico:

TABLE 7

Returns on Selected Research Investments *

Research Activity	Rate of Return (*per cent per annum*)
United States	
Hybrid corn	700 (as of 1955)
Hybrid sorghum	360 (as of 1967)
Poultry	137 (as of 1960)
Public agricultural research	300 (1954–59)
Mexico	
Wheat	750 (1943–63)
Corn	300 (1943–63)
Total agricultural research	290 (1943–63)

* As quoted in T. W. Schultz, *Economic Growth and Agriculture,* New York: McGraw-Hill, 1968, p. 85.

These estimates do not include most of the work undertaken by private agribusiness corporations. Even though many of their research results are not patentable—a newly designed haybaler can be patented, but a better method of applying fertilizer to corn cannot—they still find research profitable. As of 1966, the investment of private firms in agricultural research accounted for well over half of the total United States effort.

Perhaps the single most profitable investment in agricultural research to date is that of the Ford and Rockefeller Foundations in the International Rice Research Institute at Los Banos. The total expenditure at IRRI, including the initial investment in 1962 and the year-to-year operating costs, was $15 million as of 1968. Sterling Wortman, of the Rockefeller Foundation, estimates that the 1967–68 rice harvest in Asia was $300 million higher because of the new IRRI varieties. The figure for 1968–69 may approach a billion dollars. These figures cannot be regarded as returns on research investment alone, since the additional production costs associated with the new varieties have not been deducted. Nevertheless, it is clear that the return to society on the original investment is exceedingly high, and the benefits derived from the rices and improved production practices developed by IRRI are only beginning to appear.

The payoff on agricultural research may be potentially higher in the poor countries than in the rich. With the possibilities for expanding the cultivated area virtually exhausted in many areas, there is urgent need for new technologies to raise land productivity, both to increase the food supply and to provide a base for over-all economic development. To meet this need, researchers can draw on the backlog of scientific knowledge evolved over the past few centuries in the West. They also have ready access to the world collections of germ plasm for major cereal crops, some assembled only very recently.

Many countries are thus experiencing windfall gains in agricultural production because they are able to adopt directly technologies developed elsewhere. Pakistan and India, for example, spent very little on trials of the Mexican wheats before deciding that they were well adapted to local growing conditions. Thus these countries were able to acquire very quickly a highly advanced technology on a massive scale with a nominal outlay for research.

FORMING A GLOBAL RESEACH NETWORK

The high returns on the research that went into the new seeds could not have been realized had not the process of transferring research technology been progressively institutionalized. The process started long ago in the United States, where government, the universities, and private corporations have been complementing one another's efforts ever since the first land-grant college was chartered, the first county agent created, and the first commercial seed salesman began making his rounds. Several institutions, including international assistance agencies, foundations, multinational corporations, government agencies, and research centers, are becoming loosely linked in an informal international network which greatly facilitates the transfer of agricultural technology among countries. But it was the Rockefeller and Ford Foundations that carried the institutionalization of technological transfer a giant step forward in the development of the new seeds.

The decision by the Rockefeller and Ford Foundations to pool their resources and establish a global agricultural research network was an international event of enormous significance. Since rice is the staple food of most of the world's poor people, the foundations decided to focus their first joint research effort on rice in Asia, where 92 per cent of the world's rice crop is produced and consumed. The government of the Philippines donated the land for what became the IRRI, the Ford Foundation met the construction costs of buildings and equipment, and the Rockefeller Foundation provided the operating budget and recruited the scientists who were to organize and direct the research program. The Board of Directors was international in composition. The staff of scientists was both international and interdisciplinary. Geneticists, plant physiologists, plant pathologists, agronomists, economists, and entomologists were drawn from some 25 countries.

IRRI scientists have developed close working ties with scientists in the Philippines, Indonesia, Malaysia, Ceylon, Burma, India, Pakistan, South Vietnam, and Thailand, thus establishing an informal communications network so that the results of research at IRRI can quickly be made available to agricultural scientists everywhere. The objective of the Institute is to create a worldwide system for the continuing exchange of rice germ plasm and research results.

With the global effort to expand rice production under way, the two foundations turned their attention to wheat and corn, again combining their resources to expand the highly successful cooperative Rockefeller-Mexico effort. In 1963, Mexican scientists assumed responsibility for the Mexican program *per se,* and Ford and Rockefeller jointly established the International Corn and Wheat Improvement Center (CIMMYT in Spanish), with the encouragement of the Mexican government. Like IRRI, the Center has an international board of directors and an international staff of scientists.

Some 60,000 strains of wheat from the Mexican program and another 6,000 from the World Wheat Collection of the U.S. Department of Agriculture provide an almost unlimited source of genetic raw material for the talented staff of wheat breeders at CIMMYT. A highly selective collection of corn germ plasm has been assembled for a major effort to expand world production of this cereal, the world's third-ranking food staple and principal feed grain. Since many of the Rockefeller and Ford scientists are drawn from the ranks of the USDA and land-grant universities, these institutions maintain close working relations with research programs within the United States.

The foundations are once again pooling their resources in agricultural research. In Colombia, the International Center for Tropical Agriculture (CIAT in Spanish) has been established. CIAT, which focuses on both crops and animal production, is already producing new varieties of rice particularly suited to Latin America. A new center, to be located in Nigeria, is to focus on tropical soils as well as crops.

THE NEED FOR APPLIED RESEARCH

All of these ventures are designed to increase our understanding of agriculture in the tropics so that some of the vast unused or underused areas can be made productive. Until recently, most agricultural research programs in the tropical-subtropical countries were not only poorly financed but lacked real relevance to the needs of local farmers. They tended to be patterned after programs in the rich countries, where the emphasis is on basic research. But advancing the frontiers of knowledge is a luxury poor countries cannot afford.

Even where research had been aimed at producing practical results in these countries, the results were disappointing, in part because the research concentrated on cash crops rather than on basic food staples. An even more important factor is the lack of awareness of what had been achieved elsewhere. In Turkey, for example, the Mexican wheat seeds were pronounced unsuitable for local use at the government research stations. Had it not been for Mehmet Can Eliyesil, a venturous farmer who planted seeds smuggled into Turkey and proved the contrary, that judgment might still stand today.

The progressive institutionalization of agricultural research and the dissemination of results on a global scale means that the practical applicability of results will increasingly become the criterion for the formulation and selection of research projects in the poor countries. Economists, rarely involved in research projects until recently, will be brought in to help ensure relevance to farmers' needs. Perhaps most important, more research will be tailored to specific problems in specific localities: when and how to irrigate, when to plant, the optimum plant population, when and how to fertilize, and which pest-control practices will not adversely affect other forms of life, upsetting the ecological balance. Literally a world of experience can soon be brought to focus on these specific problems in widely differing environments.

The institutionalization of the transfer of research knowledge will both feed and be fed by the momentum of the Green Revolution. Just as the widespread use of the new technologies gives rise to a host of "second-generation problems" (discussed in Chapters 9, 10, and 11), to it gives rise to a host of second-generation research needs. The practice of year-round cropping particularly will generate new needs for applied research. The long-term maintenance of soil fertility under continuous cropping, will require a much more intimate knowledge of the effect of continuous cropping on tropical soils than currently exists.

Much more needs to be known about the possibilities for farm diversification. In which crops should a given country diversify? If a country finds itself with a surfeit of grain, what are the mechanics of expanding livestock and poultry production to absorb the grain? What incentives can governments apply to facilitate this development? These are complex, difficult questions to which answers are not easily found.

Recent gains in cereal production, as we have noted, are based largely on exogenous technologies, introduced from Mexico and the Philippines. These will not sustain rapid long-term growth in agriculture. As agricultural productivity rises, further research efforts must be initiated locally to maintain current productivity as well as advance it further.

As Stakman points out, "While man breeds new wheats, nature breeds new rusts, and occasionally she spawns virulent ones than can attack varieties that had been resistant to those previously prevalent." [1] Thus plant breeding is a never-ending process. Traditional agriculture maintains a certain level of productivity independent of research efforts, but the productivity levels of modern agriculture would decline rapidly if agricultural research were discontinued.

Spectacular though the results in cereal breeding are, many further breakthroughs, some not yet envisaged, are certain to occur as more and more resources are mobilized. The concentrated effort to share breeding materials and research results in an interconnected, systematic fashion is certain to bring handsome rewards. A good beginning has been made, but most of the benefits of this recently organized effort are reserved for the future.

---

[1] E. C. Stakman, Richard Bradfield, and Paul C. Mangelsdorf, *Campaigns Against Hunger*, Cambridge: Belknap Press, 1967, p. 76.

7

The Multinational Corporation

In the United States, the institution most responsible for the development and dissemination of agricultural technology is the private corporation. Its lusty offspring, the multinational corporation, promises to institutionalize the transfer of technology on a global scale.

During the early decades of this century, nearly all agricultural research in the United States was government-sponsored, conducted by the Department of Agriculture and the State Experiment Stations. The extension services, led by county agents, were the principal means through which the results of this research reached individual farmers.

Since World War II this picture has changed dramatically. Today most agricultural research in the United States is conducted in the laboratories and on the experimental farms of private corporations, whether these be manufacturers of farm implements or producers of fertilizers and other farm inputs. Most of the new technology reaching American farmers today comes by way of new products and the highly trained sales and service forces of these corporations. "Agribusiness" has found it very profitable to invest in research and agricultural extension. The large-scale entry of agribusiness corporations into these activities is in large measure responsible for the innovative, dynamic character of American agriculture during the past quarter century.

There is good reason to think that the same process will take place in the poor countries. As increases in farm production become more dependent upon purchased inputs, and as the proportion of farm production that is marketed rises, investment in agribusiness becomes more important. In fact, that investment must grow much faster than agricultural production itself. It is difficult to see how this needed new investment in the poor countries will be found without engaging the capital and the technical resources of the multinational corporation.

Multinational corporations transfer technology from one country to another in varied ways. The transfer may be made in the form of products, such as tractors or tillage equipment, or processes, such as feed-mixing formulae and the techniques of food processing. Or it may involve trained personnel—industrial managers, chemical engineers, agronomists. Perhaps the most important instance of the development and transfer of agricultural technology through the multinational corporations has occurred in fertilizer production.

THE FERTILIZER BREAKTHROUGH

While the plant breeders were developing new varieties of wheat and rice, chemical engineers were scoring a comparable technical breakthrough in the production of fertilizer. The key advance was made in the early 'sixties, when engineers at the M. W. Kellogg Company of Buffalo, New York, developed a more efficient process for synthesizing ammonia from atmospheric nitrogen. The new process uses huge centrifugal compressors which reduce by a third both the initial capital cost and the operating costs of ammonia plants. Because of the multinational corporations, these beneficial new nitrogen-synthesizing technologies know no boundaries.

Although the new ammonia process greatly reduces the cost of producing nitrogenous fertilizer, it presented the fertilizer industry with a difficult decision. Only very large and expensive plants can use this process. Firms in the industry had to decide whether to switch to the newer technology, replacing small plants with large ones, or face the prospect of being unable to compete in the world market. Industry opted for the new process on a large scale. Nearly all the ammonia production capacity built since 1966 is in plants designed to use the new process. This means that by 1971 the new capacity actually built or under construction will be nearly as large as was the total world ammonia capacity in 1966.

Decisions in the world fertilizer industry are, of course, influenced most by forecasts of demand in temperate-zone agriculture, where the bulk of fertilizer sales have always been made. The decision to move *en masse* to the new ammonia process reflected the expectation that temperate-zone agriculture was going to be called on to provide large amounts of food aid for the poor countries for several more years. Now that the demand for food aid is falling off markedly and the poor countries are unable to finance imports of as much fertilizer as they need, the excess of fertilizer capacity resulting from the switch to larger and more efficient plants becomes even greater. A study by the Tennessee Valley Authority estimates that demand will not catch up with production capacity until 1972.

Meanwhile, the cost of the two other basic plant nutrients, phosphate and potash, is also being reduced. New techniques of concentrating phosphates have been commercialized, lowering the cost of both manufacture and transport. New potash fields, so rich and so vast that they are expected to meet world needs for centuries to come, are now being successfully exploited in Canada.

Right now, with cereal prices still attractive and fertilizer prices declining, fertilizer use is rising at 16 per cent a year in the poor countries. This is far faster than in the rich countries, where fertilizer use is approaching saturation. The use of fertilizer in Brazil, essentially unchanged from 1960 to

1966, more than doubled in the succeeding three years. Fertilizer use in India, which increased only slowly during the early 'sixties, more than tripled from 1966 to 1969. The story in Pakistan and Turkey is much the same. Setting the stage for this rapid expansion were literally thousands of field demonstrations of fertilizer use sponsored by the Food and Agricultural Organization (FAO) of the United Nations.

The new technologies promise lower fertilizer prices in the 'seventies than prevailed in the 'sixties. To the extent that the poor countries can pay for increased imports of fertilizer, either alone or with aid funds, they will benefit. But these countries, facing shortages of foreign exchange, are also increasing their own fertilizer production capacity, often with the help of the multinational corporations.

During the mid-1960's, a number of countries, including India and Pakistan, received large loans from the United States Agency for International Development to finance imports of sorely needed fertilizer. At the same time, the United States and the World Bank put a great deal of pressure on the two governments, especially the Indian government, to encourage multinational corporations to invest in local production capacity. The Indian government changed its policy abruptly in December, 1965, to permit these firms to price and distribute their products in India. Joint ventures between Indian and foreign firms were especially encouraged.

The excess fertilizer capacity in rich countries and the insufficient supply in the poor countries pose ticklish problems. Not all countries are well positioned to strike a good balance between imports and local production. Turkey, for example, which has sharply expanded the acreage planted to high-yielding wheats, experienced a severe shortage of fertilizer in the early spring of 1969, even though it had allocated a substantial amount of scarce foreign exchange for fertilizer imports. Consequently, much of the production potential of the new wheats was not realized. This is but one example of

how the ability of the poor countries to produce or buy
fertilizer at reasonable prices can affect the future course of
the agricultural revolution. However, the ability of the multinational corporations to transfer technology rapidly and
efficiently provides real hope that this problem will be vexing
only in the short run.

Supplying Farmers' Needs

Fertilizer is only one item in the package of new inputs
which farmers need in order to realize the full potential of
the new seeds. Once it becomes profitable to use modern
technology, the demand for all kinds of farm inputs increases
rapidly. And only agribusiness firms can supply these new
inputs efficiently. This means that the multinational corporation has a vested interest in the agricultural revolution along
with the poor countries themselves.

Again, American experience provides a useful guide. Supplying farmers' needs can be big business. Farm inputs purchased by farmers in the United States totaled $21.5 billion
in 1965, of which about $9 billion consisted of feed and
livestock purchases, many from other farmers. The remaining $12.5 billion consisted of items purchased from the non-
farm or industrial sector, including fertilizer, petroleum
products, farm equipment, electricity, veterinary services, and
animal antibiotics. For each acre of the 300 million acres
they cultivate, American farmers spend $42 annually on pro-
duction inputs and services supplied by the non-farm sector.
Expenditures per acre are higher still in countries like Japan,
which practice more intensive cultivation.

Ignoring for the moment the crucial problem of foreign
exchange, we can expect a steady rise in expenditures by
farmers in the poor countries for the same sorts of inputs.
If enough foreign aid is forthcoming in the 'seventies, the
rise could be dramatic, first in the form of imported goods
and later in the form of new production capacity.

We have seen how fertilizer imports have already risen several fold in recent years in Turkey, Brazil, Pakistan, and India. Imports of other agricultural chemicals are also climbing. In Pakistan they tripled between 1961 and 1965; in Thailand they doubled in the same period. Although data are not yet available for the later half of the decade, there are indications that the increase may be even more rapid.

As we saw in Chapter 3, the new seeds have created a vast new demand for irrigation pumps and tubewells. In 1956 there were 27 firms in India manufacturing this equipment, with a total annual capacity of 67,000 pumps. In 1966, some 200,000 were produced. Meeting the estimated demand for 400,000 pumps in 1970 should mean the employment of close to a quarter of a million laborers in the production of the steel used in the pumps and in their manufacture and distribution. The growth in the number of pumps in use also means climbing requirements for both electrical power and fuel.

The use of pesticides, now becoming essential to protect the heavy capital outlays associated with high-yielding varieties, often requires high-pressure sprayers. Early-maturing rice varieties, which ripen during the monsoon, require mechanical drying before storage, since the time-honored method of spreading rice on the roadside to dry is not feasible. Both of these factors generate demand for new farm equipment.

Governments often fail to consider seriously the equipment and maintenance needs of farmers, although perhaps more often by default than by overt action. In any given developing country, easily half the farm tractors may be idle at any point in time, simply because spare parts are not available. An estimated 40 per cent of the tractors in India in 1966 were idle, mostly for this reason. Mechanical grain harvesters, imported into Brazil from Eastern Europe to use up currency balances accumulated from the export of coffee and other commodities, are now idle, again for lack of spare parts. Governments err most often when they succumb to buying farm equipment on impulse because they are offered a one-shot bargain or have some otherwise unusable currency in the bank.

Adequate maintenance systems do not exist for at least two reasons: first, farm equipment is spread so thinly that the cost of maintenance is often inordinately high. Secondly, governments have aggravated this already bad situation by permitting the import of farm equipment from several sources. This makes it virtually impossible to establish maintenance systems and stock spare parts for the many different makes and sizes of tractors and attachments.

To minimize this waste of capital, developing countries should select two or three farm-equipment manufacturing firms, preferably from different countries, and invite competition in building up a local supply and service organization. Eventually this should lead to a local farm-equipment assembling and perhaps even manufacturing industry. Foreign suppliers should be encouraged to establish native dealerships capable of supplying both custom-hire and maintenance services.

The multinational corporation is playing an important part in this expanded activity. In the Philippines, for example, Standard Oil of New Jersey (ESSO) has a highly successful program for delivering the needed inputs to farmers. ESSO has established some 400 agro-service centers to serve as marketing outlets, not only for the fertilizer produced at ESSO's plant in the Philippines, but also for other associated inputs, such as seed, pesticides, and farm implements. Manned by trained agriculturists who can provide farmers with technological advice and services, these have become one-stop shopping centers for Filipino farmers. Established just as the new varieties were catching on, they are making a strategic contribution to the striking gains in Philippine rice production.

PROCESSING FARM PRODUCTS

From the point of view of international agribusiness, many of the promising new investment opportunities are in the area of processing farm products or using them as raw materials in manufacturing. Rice milling, sugar refining, fruit and vegetable canning, vegetable-oil extracting, feed mixing, and textile manufacturing are examples of agriculturally related industries which benefit from the modernization of agriculture.

A lack of processing industries often imposes unnecessary constraints on a country's agricultural development. This could become even more serious in the future as poor countries reach self-sufficiency in cereals and seek ways of using land no longer needed to produce these food staples. Developing countries can obtain the necessary technological and marketing know-how by encouraging multinational agricultural processing and manufacturing firms to invest locally.

A recent example of such an effort, initiated by a private corporation doing a worldwide business, is the Overseas Agricultural Development Corporation, formed in Japan to supply farm inputs and technical assistance to developing countries. Some 24 Japanese firms are participating. They have projects under way or planned in Indonesia, Thailand, Cambodia, and Malaysia. The basic objective is to increase the production of feed grains, oilseeds, and other farm products for shipment to Japan, thus expanding overseas markets for Japanese agricultural equipment, fertilizer, and other farm requisites.

A specific effort to accomplish similar objectives is a Japanese-Indonesian agreement to encourage the cultivation and improve the quality of corn. The government of East Java is planning an additional 250,000 tons of corn production annually for export, primarily through the use of fertilizer on irrigated land. Joint efforts are under way to improve drying, warehousing, transport, and port facilities.

A joint Sino-Japanese meat-processing plant was opened in 1968 in Taiwan. During the first five months, it exported to Japan more than two million pounds of choice cuts of frozen pork. Exports were then halted temporarily because of pork shortages and rising prices but are expected to resume once pork production catches up with demand. Much of this pork is being produced with imported feed grains, largely from the United States.

In the Uraba Valley of Colombia, the United Fruit Company is working with farmers to develop a new banana-producing area. The company does not own the farms but acts as the marketing agent and technical adviser for some 260 privately owned farms. It arranges production credit from an American bank, guarantees a minimum purchase price for the bananas, and provides technical assistance in improving quality. The price differential between first- and second-quality bananas in the European market is such that a very high portion of the crop must be of first quality or the entire enterprise will fail. A high level of technology distinguishes this enterprise from the standards that generally prevail in the production and marketing of most farm products in Colombia. Perhaps the most strategic contribution United Fruit is making to the Colombian operation is in providing access to external markets through its global marketing system.

Pineapple enterprises in poor countries offer another example of production stimulated by multinational food-processing firms with global marketing networks. The expansion of pineapple production in the Philippines from barely 100,-000 tons in 1960 to more than 200,000 tons nine years later is due in large measure to investments in processing facilities by such firms as Dole. By investing in canning and freezing facilities in Mexico, multinational food-processing firms are capitalizing on both that country's favorable climate and underemployed labor force and the lucrative North American market for processed fruit and vegetables.

These are but a few illustrations of how multinational corporations stimulate both the development and the diversification of agriculture in the poor countries, linking their unused or underused resources with markets elsewhere in the world.

NATIONALISM AND THE MULTINATIONAL FIRM

Given the pre-eminence of the multinational corporation in international development, it is surprising that it is accorded so little attention in development literature. In part, this may reflect the fact that many of the basic concepts of development were formulated before the emergence, relatively recently, of the multinational corporation as a major factor in development.

Although there are occasional, highly publicized instances of expropriation, limited largely to extractive industries, foreign private investment is growing rapidly. According to the *Survey of Current Business,* American private investment abroad totaled $17 billion in 1930 and had reached only $19 billion by 1950 but then began to climb rapidly, rising to $50 billion in 1960 and $87 billion in 1966. Overseas investments of European and Japanese firms are also expanding. Although only a small share of this total investment is in the poor countries, it is growing. So too is the share going into manufacturing as opposed to extractive industries.

Apart from the fact that the multinational firm's contribution to development is difficult to separate out, much of its developmental impact is concentrated during the middle and late 'sixties, too recent to measure. Thus far, only a small fraction of the overseas investment of multinational corporations has been allotted to agribusiness in the poor countries. But the amount is increasing. Sales of farm inputs and opportunities for new investment in food processing and related activities are increasing in the poor countries in close relation to the acreage planted to the high-yielding varieties.

In the 1970's, agribusiness investment by private multination firms in some poor countries could far surpass that going into extractive industries and thus be much more welcome, because it would more directly stimulate local industrial activity and create employment.

There is a challenge here to both the mutinational corporations and the poor countries. The former, in their pursuit of ever more efficient combinations of raw materials, labor, management, and markets, have to demonstrate an interest in the local economy. They have to be truly multinational investors, not just foreign investors. They have to be willing to invest for the long haul, not just for the quick result.

The poor countries, on the other hand, have to try to "denationalize" the subject of agribusiness investment and treat it for what it is: an amazingly efficient way of institutionalizing the transfer of technical knowledge in agriculture. The agricultural revolution provides the setting for a more pragmatic approach to a touchy issue.

Bertolt Brecht offers the reasoning for such an approach in these lines from his *Threepenny Opera:*

"Now all you gentlemen who wish to lead us,
To teach us to resist from mortal sin,
Your prior obligation is to feed us:
When we've had our lunch, your preaching can begin."

8

The Role of the United States Government

In his annual foreign-aid message to the Congress in May, 1969, President Nixon declared:

> A few years ago, mass starvation within a decade seemed clearly possible in many poor nations. Today they stand at least on the threshold of a dramatic breakthrough in food production. The combination of the new "miracle seeds" for wheat and rice, . . . fertilizer, . . . improved cultivation practices, and constructive agricultural policies shows what is possible. They also demonstrate the potential for success when foreign aid, foreign private investment, and domestic resources in developing countries join together in a concentrated attack on poverty.

A lot of foreigners and a lot of foreign aid went into the making of the agricultural revolution, but American institutions provided by far the largest contribution, whether measured in terms of men or of money. And American foreign aid was centrally involved.

The role of the American government in helping to transfer the technologies that made the agricultural breakthrough posssible can be compared to the role that the American government played in the Marshall Plan. Indeed, if the agricul-

tural revolution maintains its momentum into the 1970's—
and if the United States continues its support—our contribution could exceed our earlier contribution to the postwar
recovery of Western Europe. Certainly the number of people
affected will be several times greater.

Ironically, the American contribution to the agricultural
revolution was made at a time when "foreign aid" was falling
into disrepute, from which it has not yet recovered. In the
mid-'sixties, when food aid and fertilizer was being shipped
to the poor countries at an annual cost of more than $1.5
billion, the Congress and many citizens were becoming disenchanted with foreign aid. Many, no doubt, were disillusioned by the fact that the poor countries could not be
"modernized" with the dispatch and efficiency with which
reconstruction had proceeded in Western Europe under the
Marshall Plan, as though the two situations were in any way
comparable. In any case, as the Agency for International Development (AID) became progressively involved in Vietnam
and its operations were more and more bent to the purposes
of war, support for foreign aid declined to its present nadir.

This is not the place to review all the aspects of the debate
over foreign aid. However, the role that the Agency for International Development played in helping to transfer the
technologies that made the agricultural revolution possible
needs to be spelled out. How the President and the Congress
decide to dispose of the question of foreign aid once Vietnam
ceases to be the preoccupation that it is today will have a
significant effect on the momentum of the agricultural revolution in the 1970's.

USAID

In the unlovely language of the bureaucracy, something
called "USAID" has been very much in evidence in the countryside of the poor nations of the world for the past 15 years.
Food aid, amounting to one third of the aid effort, has

been most prominent. Since the Bengal famine of 1943, which took an estimated three million lives, there has been no major famine in the world; American food aid is part of the reason. For several years during the 'sixties, food aid was feeding an estimated 100 million people a year—half the current population of the United States

Food aid not only fed people; it also generated local funding for development projects in agriculture such as rural credit systems and grain storage facilities, which could be carried out with little or no foreign exchange. And, as we saw in Chapter 1, when the United States shifted to a "short tether" policy under which food aid was committed in terms of months rather than years, there was an immediate response from leaders who had been trying to give agriculture higher priority in their development programs.

The next largest share of aid for agriculture went to help finance the rural infrastructure—the farm-to-market roads, irrigation projects, and rural electric systems—that was a necessary precondition for the successful introduction of the new seeds. Fertilizer imports financed by AID helped to meet the soaring demand that came when several countries began to adopt the new seeds. AID provided investment assistance in the form of loans and investment guarantees to American corporations that collaborated with local firms in fertilizer production ventures.

New program-management concepts introduced in some countries by AID technicians made the dissemination of the new seeds much more rapid than it would otherwise have been. Turkey and Vietnam, which are learning how to use the new management tools, have benefitted immensely. Very few people in late 1966 would have predicted that it would be possible for Turkey, within less than a year, to increase the number of farmers using Mexican wheats from 100 to 50,000 and, within less than two years, to 200,000. Vietnam's accelerated rice-production program, launched only weeks before the Tet offensive in early 1968, stayed on schedule despite the widespread disruption and devastation. In the summer of 1967, there were only a few test plots of IR-8 in South Vietnam. By late summer of 1968 more than 20,000 farmers had successfully harvested IR-8 crops with yields double those of local varieties.

AID also financed a large force of technical-assistance experts whose contribution has been incalculable. Some were hired by AID itself; some came from the United States Department of Agriculture; some from the universities; some from other private organizations. These technicians worked on such varied problems as irrigation, plant pest control, grain storage, and credit and marketing organizations.

The decision of AID Administrator David Bell and Secretary of Agriculture Orville Freeman to pool the technical resources of their respective agencies greatly expanded the work financed by AID. An International Agricultural Development Service was established in USDA that could draw from the USDA's 29,000 professional agriculturists to fill requests made to and by AID. Staff of USDA's Agricultural Research Service, Soil Conservation Service, Farmer Cooperative Service, and other agencies were all enlisted in the cause of the agricultural revolution abroad.

At the same time, a liaison office was established between AID and the land-grant universities. From 1956 to 1966, 35 rural-development contracts were signed by AID and various land-grant universities. The focus in each case is on institution building in one or more of three areas—education, research, and/or extension. Most contracts are focused on efforts to create an agricultural university, in the land-grant university tradition of service to the rural community.

A good example is the University of Tennessee's contract in India, which extends back some 15 years. One of five universities with contracts in India, Tennessee is working with the Mysore University of Agricultural Sciences. Tennessee faculty members on assignment in India advise several departments in curriculum development and research programs.

Kansas State, the University of Illinois, Ohio State University, and the University of Missouri have similar relationships with host universities in other states within India. Over the past decade and a half, these universities, through their advising, teaching, and faculty exchanges, have contributed enormously to the growing competence of Indian agricultural universities in teaching and research, and to the ability of these institutions to develop and disseminate new technology.

Lessons Learned

There is no use pretending that the many involvements of the United States government in agricultural development in the poor countries have been of uniformly high quality or uniformly successful. Mistakes have been made, sometimes serious ones. But lessons have been learned, too, and the Americans involved have proved that their native inventiveness is useful even in cultural environments very different from their own.

One important lesson learned is that we Americans, with our great wealth and energy, can stifle initiative in others and discourage the very acts of self-help that are needed most. This was one initial result of our food-aid policy in such countries as India, even where that aid helped to stave off mass starvation in the recipient country as well as to get rid of unwanted agricultural surpluses here at home. And India was not the only country in which we made this mistake. This is a good example of how we can do positive harm abroad if we base our policies on a narrow, short-run interpretation of our own economic interests.

In learning this lesson, we helped to establish the primacy of price policy in agricultural development, even in poor countries. We knew from our own experience that farmers would use modern technology only if convinced that it was profitable for them to do so. We believed that this would be equally true of the peasant farmers in poor countries, even though they were illiterate and tradition-bound. Secretary Freeman was fond of saying, "I've met many farmers who couldn't read or write, but never one who couldn't count." However, until the governments of poor countries were willing to provide incentives to peasant farmers in order to increase production, it was not possible to refute convincingly those who persisted in believing that the peasant farmer in tradition-bound societies was somehow indifferent to money incentives or unable to respond to them in a productive way.

We learned, too, that a great deal of time and money can be wasted by trying to tackle the whole spectrum of agricultural problems in a given country at once. Perhaps the single greatest constraint on agricultural development is the severely limited administrative capability of governments in aid-recipient countries. Too often in the past, our assistance in effect overtaxed this limited capability because priorities were not established.

We learned to concentrate on specific areas, such as the staple food—wheat in Turkey, rice in the Philippines. We found it much easier to get the support of national leaders, for sharply focused programs of special importance. We learned that the commitment of national leaders outside as well as inside government is essential to progress in agriculture, and that commitments were more readily given when there was a clearly defined objective in view.

Concentrating resources on limited objectives also has the highly desirable psychological effect of enabling both American technicians and their counterparts abroad to measure their progress against established goals. And, needless to say, the ability to measure results against specific goals is very useful in persuading finance ministers and budget officers of the usefulness of programs—to say nothing of legislative bodies, such as the United States Congress!

Finally, in a thousand different ways we are learning to talk effectively across cultural as well as linguistic barriers, again only after making many, many mistakes. One example must serve.

Perhaps the two most basic obstacles to the spread of new technologies in the poor countries are illiteracy and inadequate marketing systems. While working in El Salvador several years ago, two Americans, farmer-consultant Roswell Garst, of Iowa, and AID technician Benjamin Birdsall, hit on the idea of putting together in one small packet all the basic inputs needed to enable a farmer to try out a new variety on, say, a 100′ × 100′ plot in the corner of his field. If the farmer couldn't read the instructions on the packet, he had to find someone who could. But because he got all the inputs at the same time, he did not have to rely on the vagaries of the local marketing system. He had everything he needed to try out the new variety, evaluate its performance, and compare it with his traditional crop.

The packet idea spread from El Salvador to the Philippines, Vietnam, India, and elsewhere. In the Philippines, where the packets were used on a massive scale, a typical packet might contain two pounds of IR-8 rice, 42 pounds of fertilizer, and six pounds of pesticides. The idea was used not only by governments, but it has even been picked up by fertilizer companies, which have sold the packets commercially.

FUTURE CONTRIBUTION OF THE UNITED STATES

A predominant share of the world's pool of trained agricultural talent is found within the United States. American agribusiness firms and research stations are by far the most active and innovative. The future course of the agricultural revolution will therefore depend heavily on the ability and willingness of Americans to continue to contribute.

It would be nice to be able to say that when it comes to transferring agricultural technologies in the 'seventies, we could rest content with the growing global network of research activities and the growing investments in the poor countries of the multinational corporations—in short, that we could look forward to a gradual withering away of the United States government's financial aid.

However, as subsequent chapters will show in detail, agricultural development is a long way from being self-sustaining, even where the new technologies have been adopted most enthusiastically. A dynamic, fast-changing farm sector needs more technical guidance than a traditional, static one. And in many parts of the world—for example, in sub-Saharan Africa and much of Latin America—agriculture is still moving backward relative to the population rise and to growth in other sectors.

What we can say, what the distinguished members of the Pearson Commission in fact did say in their report to President McNamara of the World Bank,[1] is that the new breakthroughs in agriculture permit the poor countries to raise their sights to higher rates of economic growth in the 'seventies than those that prevailed in the 'sixties. We can say, too, to those who have become disillusioned with our overseas assistance programs, that their lack of confidence is misplaced. While they have been concentrating on our unhappy military adventure in Vietnam, something of much greater historical importance has been going on, thanks in no small part to the combined efforts of many American organizations. The breakthrough in food production and the lessons we have learned from it ought to restore our confidence that we can marshal our resources in behalf of the world's poor and hungry, with the prospect of some very encouraging results.

We can, in the 'seventies, build a new era in international

[1] Commission on International Development, *Partners in Development,* New York: Praeger, 1969.

cooperation and development on the basis of the new agricultural breakthroughs. Or we can "disengage" and merely wait for the long-term effects of such disengagement to come home to roost. Our choice will depend on how well we understand both the problems and the opportunities that lie ahead.

III

Second-Generation Problems

9

Seeds of Instability

In December, 1968, in Tanjore, one of India's model agricul-tural-development districts, 42 persons were burned to death in a tragic clash between two groups of landless laborers. They were fighting over how best to get a share of the benefits from the new seeds being planted by landowners in the district. One group was willing to work at prevailing wage rates; the other wanted to enforce a boycott against the farms where the new seeds were being planted until landlords agreed to raise wages and share some of the handsome profits that were being realized with those who owned no land.[1]

This incident illustrates how the agricultural revolution can lose some of its momentum in countries using the new seeds. A whole host of "second generation" problems has already arisen. Clifton Wharton aptly entitled an article dealing with some of these problems "The Green Revolution: Cornucopia or Pandora's Box?"[2] But fundamentally, the progress and ultimate contribution of the Revolution will be determined by how its benefits are shared.

Eugene Black, former President of the World Bank, has observed that economic development "is a fickle process; it destroys old habits and attitudes toward life and work even as it creates new opportunities: it often raises hopes much faster than the level of satisfactions." The introduction of

[1] *New York Times,* December 28, 1968, p. 3.
[2] *Foreign Affairs,* April, 1969.

77

the new seeds is bearing out this observation on a grand scale. They not only double the level of production over the levels of local varieties, but in doing so they often triple or quadruple profits. Millions of farmers have suddenly found themselves earning incomes that they had not dreamed were possible. The aspirations of millions of others, especially rural laborers without land, are being aroused in the process. As the new seeds and the associated new technologies spread, they introduce rapid and sweeping changes, creating a wave of expectations throughout society and placing great pressure on the existing social order and political system.

Conflicts are bound to arise between landowners and tenants, and between both of these groups and landless laborers. Conflicts will also arise between regions within a country where conditions in one prove more adaptable to the new technologies than do conditions in another. Most important, conflicts are bound to arise over the division of benefits between the countryside and the cities.

REGIONAL DISPARITIES

Regional disparities, often due to geographical factors, become particularly acute as the new seeds spread. Reed Hertford, in his study of Mexico,[3] divides the country into two distinct regions, north and south of a hypothetical line drawn through the center. Below the line, where approximately one third of Mexico's rural population lives, 75–80 per cent of the labor force depends on agriculture, but farm mechanization is negligible, fertilizer is still a novelty, farm wages are scarcely a third as high as those in the north, and a greater proportion of the rural population is illiterate. While increases in yields for Mexico as a whole since 1940 have been among the highest

[3] R. Hertford, *The Measured Sources of Growth of Mexican Agricultural Production and Productivity,* Washington, D.C.: U.S. Department of Agriculture, December, 1968.

in the world, yields have not increased appreciably in the area south of Mr. Hertford's line.

There is no mystery here, although there is a constant threat of trouble. To the north, the agricultural area is in many respects simply an extension of the large, irrigated farms of Arizona and California. Yields of wheat, cotton, and corn place high in world rankings. Over the past 25 years, progress in this region has taken it out of the "underdeveloped" class.

In an effort to redistribute wealth, the Mexican government recently introduced lower support prices for wheat in irrigated districts, where conditions are exceptionally favorable for high yields. Its scientists have urged more research on corn production and greater attention to the needs of the small farmer in order to increase productivity in the south. But these measures have been far from adequate.

Asian societies are experiencing similarly serious problems of regional disequilibrium as the new seeds are introduced. The problems will probably be most severe where the supply and control of water varies widely from region to region, such as in Turkey and Pakistan.

In Turkey, where wheat is the leading crop, the planting of high-yielding dwarf varieties is concentrated in the high-rainfall coastal lowlands. As farmers on the coast double their production using the new wheats, prices are likely to decline, leaving the dryland wheat farmer on the Anatolian Plateau in even worse circumstances than he is in now. The Turkish government, with the help of AID, is anticipating this problem by attempting to develop and introduce new varieties and cultural practices that will help the farmers on the dry plateau. At the same time they are making efforts to channel production increases into the development of a livestock industry, thereby creating a new market for grain. The success of this effort to diversify agriculture may determine the political and social stability of the Turkish nation in the years immediately ahead.

The widening gap in rural prosperity between East and West Pakistan helped to undermine the authority of President Ayub Khan in 1968, leading to a period of considerable political turmoil in that country. The spread of the new varieties in East Pakistan, primarily a rice-growing area, has proceeded at a snail's pace because of a lack of water control; East Pakistan has one of the highest rates of rainfall in the world, but there has been very little effort as yet to impound water and control it through effective irrigation systems. The new rices will not survive in the flooded fields where most of East Pakistan's crop is grown.

West Pakistan, on the other hand, was ideally prepared for the introduction of the new seeds from the point of view of water control. Although West Pakistan is a region of low rainfall, nearly all the cropland is irrigated, and a considerable effort has been made to exploit underground water resources through tubewells and lift pumps. In West Pakistan, therefore, acreage planted to the new varieties expanded from a few hundred in 1965 to six million in 1969. The new seeds have transformed West Pakistan from a region of acute scarcity and heavy imports of food to one of surpluses and unprecedented prosperity, while East Pakistan has continued to be a food-deficit area, hard pressed to keep food production abreast of population growth.

Water control is therefore a key to the future wellbeing of Pakistan. A major political challenge to any Pakistani government in the years ahead is bound to be that posed by the need for much greater investment in agriculture in East Pakistan relative to West Pakistan.

THE CITY AND THE COUNTRYSIDE

Agricultural price policy strongly affects the nature and direction of agricultural development. Among other things, it determines how the benefits of progress in agriculture are to be shared between the cities and the countryside. As the new technologies heighten expectations among farmers and city dwellers alike, food prices are certain to become an increasingly tendentious issue.

Governments in the poor countries can be expected to rise and fall over this isssue in the years immediately ahead. If price supports are set too high, they may provide production incentives and higher incomes to farmers, but at the same time they will create social discontent among city dwellers, whose food costs will rise. If supports are set at a lower level, most of the cost benefits of the new technologies will be passed on to the consumer, but the farmer may be unable to afford the inputs needed to exploit the new seeds.

There are many intermediate positions, of course, and finding the right price level is likely to be one of the most difficult tasks facing the governments of countries where the new seeds are being widely planted. The countryside has been the principal beneficiary for the past few years. This is fortunate, for the rural populations in these countries are among the world's poorest. As long as food is scarce, the countryside will probably continue to be the principal beneficiary, but as food production expands and a country approaches or reaches self-sufficiency, prices will be depressed unless markets can be developed abroad. Unless agricultural products can be exported, the flow of future benefits from the new technologies will be imperiled. As we shall see, the policies of the rich countries will be an important factor determining whether the new seeds are in fact seeds of orderly progress and change or seeds of instability.

With millions of farmers entering the commercial market for the first time on the wave of the new technologies, there is bound to be much disappointment and chaos. Those entering the market during periods of scarcity and exceptionally high prices will have their appetites whetted by a level of income and of living far higher than they dared dream even a few years earlier. But they must now contend with the vicissitudes of the market as well as the vagaries of weather. When the expanding food supply weakens prices, they are certain to be disappointed and to demand redress from their government. Discontent arising from unsatisfied expectations will probably be a prevalent feature of life in the 1970's in countries where the new seeds are being planted extensively.

Sharing the Wealth

All technological innovation leads in some degree to these kinds of disruption. What is different about the introduction of the new seeds is the quantum jump in technology that they represent. In Western Europe, the United States, and Japan, agricultural modernization proceeded much more gradually, and it took place in societies that were accustomed to and expected continual technological change. The new seeds are being introduced abruptly on a massive scale in societies still practicing essentially Biblical agriculture. Centuries of technological progress are being compressed into decades and, in some extreme cases, into years. Herein lies the trauma of the agricultural revolution.

A new "rich" class of farmers is bound to arise, comprised of those who have proximity to markets, or ready access to fertilizer, or who can afford to mechanize. It is to be hoped that a new entrepreneurial class will also arise as a result of the greatly expanded opportunities in agribusiness. But others will be left behind, and some who have had positions of power and wealth will lose those positions.

By creating a vast leap in the aspirations of millions of poor people and at the same time altering the relative prosperity of groups in the established order, the new seeds will inevitably cause great frustration and restlessness. They are likely to be a greater force for change than any technology or ideology ever introduced into the poor countries. The next few chapters discuss some of the challenges facing government policy-makers whose decisions will determine whether the new seeds lead to violence or to orderly change in the structure of society.

For those in the rich countries who believe in "progress," this unfolding drama has many lessons. Even the rich countries today have serious development problems, rooted in the desire of all peoples to share in the benefits of economic progress. The rich countries are finding that when aspirations are aroused, and the relative prosperity of various groups in society begins to change, the resulting dissatisfactions may lead to violence. We can no longer pretend that the notion of "development" is peculiar to poor or tropical countries. It is, rather, the common denominator of the human predicament today. How to share the benefits of economic growth between rich and poor without in the process shutting those benefits off is a problem that transcends all geographical and political boundaries. It poses a basic question for all mankind: Can we manage progress or not?

10

Overloaded Marketing Systems

During April and May of 1968, scores of village schools closed in northern India. The reason was not student unrest or a teachers' strike. It was that schoolhouses were the only uninhabited buildings capable of storing a record crop of wheat that had already overwhelmed all other local storage facilities. The classrooms were filled to the ceiling with the new grain, and even that wasn't enough room. The overflow was finally stored in the open, unprotected from the weather. The bumper harvest was 35 per cent greater than the previous record crop! A race began to get it to New Delhi and other cities where there were empty grain elevators before the monsoon rains came. Fortunately, the rains were late, and the exposed grain was safely loaded in boxcars.

The most immediate obstacle to the agricultural revolution is the woefully inadequate state of marketing systems in countries where the new seeds are being planted. This is not surprising. Investment tends to concentrate on production, a much more tangible process than marketing. Since 1960, some development-assistance organizations (particularly the World Bank) have attempted to improve marketing. But it has been a slow and tedious process. A close look at the marketing situation provides insight into some of the "second generation" problems of the Green Revolution.

THE MARKETING MULTIPLIER

With the new technologies, farmers' marketable surpluses of cereals have increased far faster, proportionately, than production. A farmer who is accustomed to marketing a fifth of his wheat harvest finds his marketable surplus tripled when his crop suddenly increases 40 per cent. Even after retaining more for home consumption, as many are doing, farmers who have doubled their output with the new seeds are increasing their marketable surpluses several fold.

When the wheat harvest is suddenly 35 per cent greater than the previous record, as was the case in India in 1968, the marketable surpluses are bound to overwhelm all the components of the marketing system—storage, transport, grading, and processing operations and the local market intelligence system. In West Pakistan, land planted to the new IR-8 rice rose from 10,000 acres to nearly a million *in one year* (1967–1968); West Pakistan suddenly found itself with an exportable surplus of rice, but without the processing, transport, and pricing facilities needed to handle an export trade efficiently.

Four consecutive annual increases in the rice harvest in the Philippines are creating another kind of market crisis: a pressing need for more drying and warehousing facilities. In the Philippines, not only is the crop considerably larger, but the new, early-maturing rices must be harvested during the monsoon. Traditional methods of drying rice—in the sun along the roadside—are no longer feasible; farmers must use mechanical grain driers to dry the rice en route from the field to the storage bin.

The Green Revolution found some countries with marketing systems oriented to a considerable extent toward handling imported grain. Over the past 15 years, many large coastal cities in Asia, including Bombay, Karachi, Calcutta, and Djakarta, have been living literally from ship-to-mouth for

extended periods off the wheat shipped each year under the
United States food-aid program. In the mid-'sixties these
shipments averaged 450 million bushels yearly. Systems designed to move food surpluses from the countryside to the
cities or to other food-deficit areas atrophied from disuse.

THE MARKETING GAP

The technologies used in food production by progressive
farmers in both rich and poor countries are quite similar,
even though the size of operations may vary widely. The more
advanced farmers everywhere use improved seeds, chemical
fertilizer, and pesticides. But when it comes to marketing the
production, the technological gap is enormous.

One way of measuring the gap in grain marketing is to
compare techniques in India and the United States. Both
countries have the same area of cropland, roughly 340 million
acres. On this land India has 60 million farmers, nearly all of
them producing grain. The United States has three million
farmers, of whom perhaps two million are grain producers.

In India, grain changes hands in small quantities, initially
between the farmer and the local grain merchant. The negotiations, often quite prolonged, usually take place with the
buyer personally feeling, smelling, and sometimes even tast-
ing the grain. Often the transaction involves only a few sacks
of grain.

In the United States, grain is scientifically graded as it
leaves the farm for such attributes as cleanliness (percentage
of foreign material) and moisture and protein content. It is
then classified according to detailed specifications established
by government marketing agencies and, on the basis of this
classification, moves through the marketing system.

Vast quantities of grain are bought and sold in the United
States without being seen by either buyer or seller. Transac-
tions are often conducted solely on paper. Frequently, those

who are buying the grain do not even know where it is located, only where it is to be delivered. This level of efficiency is possible only if there are grades and standards that buyers and sellers have confidence in and adhere to.

The effects of this difference between the two systems are hard to quantify but can be illustrated. In 1966, James Boulware, United States Department of Agriculture Attaché in New Delhi, tried to determine from various research reports just how much of India's grain crop was lost during the successive stages of marketing. In one report he found figures showing that grain losses to rodents amounted to 50 per cent; in another, he found figures claiming that 15 per cent was lost during milling and processing; one report claimed that 15 per cent was lost to cows, birds, and monkeys; still another attributed a loss of 10 per cent to insect damage; and, finally, he cited figures purporting to show a loss of 15 per cent in storage and transit. He solemnly concluded that there was no mystery about India's food deficit; 105 per cent of the crop was lost in the marketing process!

If nothing else, Mr. Boulware's survey proved that it is difficult to get reliable data on the efficiency of traditional marketing systems; this difficulty contributes to the disinterest in marketing.

INVESTMENT IN MARKETING

The course of the Green Revolution will be influenced to an important degree by the amount and effectiveness of new investment in marketing farm products in the tropical countries in the years immediately ahead. This is an area in which international cooperation can have a profound effect.

We saw in Chapter 7 that there will be vast new investment opportunities in the business of processing farm commodities. But investment will be needed quite as much in other components of the marketing system—storage, transportation, grades and standards, and market intelligence.

Subsistence agriculture is independent of transport systems; only when farmers enter the marketplace do transport systems become important. Commercial agriculture very often begins with the establishment of a transportation link—a new highway or a new water-transport service.

Over the past decade and more, AID, the World Bank, and other development assistance agencies have loaned hundreds of millions of dollars for "farm-to-market roads." These investments probably account for a significant part of the increase in agricultural exports that has taken place recently in the tropical countries.

A good example is the new highway between the inland city of Curitiba, in Brazil, and Paranagua, on the coast. The highway was built to improve the links between the country's vast agricultural hinterland and the world market. This project of the Brazilian government also included deepening the port and reducing or eliminating export taxes on selected farm exports, such as corn. Unfortunately, there are all too few such examples in Latin America. It is doubtful that any region has paid so dearly for inadequacies in its agricultural marketing system. In the 'sixties, world trade in feed grains and soybeans nearly doubled, but Latin America, potentially a large exporter of both, remained on the sidelines. Despite vast resources of both land and water, most Latin American countries have made little effort to link these assets with the world market.

The Friendship Highway from Bangkok to Korat, in Thailand, is another dramatic example of what a highway can do to agriculture. It was not built primarily as a farm-to-market road but, rather, to give quick access to Thailand's vulnerable northeast provinces, where Communist insurgents have been active. Nonetheless, the highway helped Thailand, traditionally a one-crop (rice) exporter, to become a ranking world exporter of corn. Actually, Thailand in 1968 exported more corn than rice. This was possible in part because the Friendship Highway linked large areas of fertile, virgin soil with Bangkok and the world market.

Storage is a crucial element in any marketing system; it becomes much more so as the new seeds spread. The shortage of storage facilities in traditional societies contributes to the wide seasonal price fluctuations, often as much as 100 per cent in a given year. The lack of on-farm storage is costly to individual farmers, who must frequently sell part of their crop at harvest, only to buy some of it back later in the year at a much higher price. The same is occasionally true of nations as well. In years of bumper harvest, countries may be forced to export at harvest time simply because storage facilities cannot hold the entire harvest. Iran exported wheat in 1968 for precisely this reason.

Storage is also needed for farm inputs, such as fertilizer and pesticides. Without adequate storage dispersed throughout the countryside, it may not be possible to assure timely deliveries of these items to large numbers of small-holder farmers.

Less costly but no less important are systems of grades and standards and of market intelligence. The latter is perhaps the more important. Buyers and sellers can act rationally only if a system exists to provide data on weather, crop conditions, crop production, production prospects, forecasts of demand, and, of course, prices. The lack of a market intelligence system often results in the simultaneous existence of scarcity and glut in different parts of a country, even where relatively efficient transportation is available. A country needs to know what its surplus of a given foodstuff is likely to be so that it will know how much it can safely export. Unless it has a fair estimate, it may be forced to wait until the next harvest to determine the excess over domestic needs. This can be costly since it both limits the exporter's ability to take advantage of seasonal price fluctuations and raises storage costs. The Philippines, Peru, and Brazil have recently established simple market news services, which have led to a noticeable decrease in waste.

If one could add up the investment needed in marketing in countries using the new seeds, the total would be large indeed —in the billions of dollars. There is no more pressing need in agriculture in the poor countries today.

The case for international cooperation in marketing is particularly strong; considerable outside assistance is going to be needed. Here, national and international development-assistance agencies can help. Perhaps the World Bank or AID should single out the marketing problem for attention over the next decade and gear their lending activities to its solution. Technical assistance to establish grades and standards and to organize market news services would be a key feature in such a program. Experienced experts in these fields are at best scarce and often simply not available at all in the poor countries.

Governments in the poor countries, AID, and the multilateral assistance agencies must address marketing with a sense of urgency matching that required to achieve the explosive gains in food production. Without such an effort, many of the potential production gains may evaporate.

I I

Other Clouds on the Horizon

In the real political life of our times, most of the "second-generation problems" to which the new technologies are giving birth will not be treated in isolation but as part of the human predicament. They will be submerged in the more general problems of sharing the benefits of technology, of creating new employment opportunities, of dealing with "urbanization" and the basic dimensions of poverty, such as malnutrition.

But there are some second-generation problems, technical and economic, that would not exist in their present form had it not been for the new technologies. Without attempting to provide an exclusive review, we shall describe how the new seeds bring with them the threat of new plant diseases, how they affect consumer tastes, and how they give rise to new economic constraints even as they remove some old ones. These, of course, are the problems of success, their seriousness often reflecting the magnitude of the successes achieved.

THE IRISH-FAMINE BACKDROP

One of the major risks of trying to establish a plant variety in an environment differing from that in which it was developed is that the new variety may fall prey to a disease to which it has no resistance. The classic example is the Irish potato famine of the late 1840's. Ireland had become dependent for

91

its food supply on the lowly potato that had been introduced from the New World. The potato proved susceptible to blight; as the result of devastating crop losses, a million and a half Irishmen died of starvation, and even greater numbers of the survivors emigrated to the United States in ensuing decades. Famine and emigration, plus delayed marriages and low birth rates over the century and a quarter since the famine, have reduced Ireland's population to four million—just half of what it was when the potato blight hit.

The potato does not readily contract blight; the temperature and humidity, among other factors, have to be exactly right—or, rather, wrong. But when these very specific conditions occur, the crop failure can be total. The same is true of wheat rust and some other diseases attacking cereals. Since the 34 million acres of high-yielding cereals in Asia is planted largely to exogenous varieties, the disease threat is particularly acute. The new wheats, developed in Mexico, are rather resistant to the wheat rusts currently prevalent in Mexico, but not necessarily to those found on the opposite side of the globe.

Rice seems to be more plagued by disease than wheat, in part because it is grown in a warmer, moister environment, more conducive to the spread of diseases. To achieve optimal yields with the new varieties, the density of the plant population is invariably increased. Aggravated by the results of heavy fertilization, which brings lush vegetative growth, this "crowding" creates ideal conditions for plant epidemics and infestations of pests, much as similar crowding does in human society. The dominant disease of rice in Asia is rice blast, a disease that occurs more frequently as the use of nitrogen fertilizer and the density of the vegetative growth increases.

While the threat of new diseases is real, there is much more preventive technology in the research bank today than when the potato blight struck in Ireland. As the exogenous varieties are crossed with local strains, the risk of a widespread outbreak of disease is reduced. At the same time, a greater number of new varieties is being used, and sources of germ plasm are becoming more diverse.

As the new varieties and associated technologies are adopted, the economics as well as the biology of disease control changes. The greater prospective returns make it feasible to institute the pest-control measures that the new biology demands. For example, the stem borer, which often causes crop losses of 10–20 per cent, can be controlled only by chemical means; with yields of one ton per acre, it may not pay to buy the needed insecticide, but with yields of three tons it becomes very profitable to do so.

Consumer Resistance

Plant breeders also have to contend with consumer resistance. Newly introduced varieties are rarely as acceptable as those which they replace and to which people are accustomed. The Mexican wheats, for example, are predominantly red wheats, but Indians and Pakistanis prefer amber wheats. The cooking qualities of IR-8 rice are invariably less popular than those of local varieties. The new rice is more chalky and is brittle, yielding more broken grains during milling.

Consumer resistance is reflected in the lower prices the new varieties command in the marketplace. Mexican wheats in Turkey sell for 10 per cent less than local wheats; we saw earlier that the price for the new rice in the Phillipines was 30 per cent below that of traditional varieties. In Pakistan, wholesalers and millers have been reluctant to buy IR-8 at all because of its milling and cooking characteristics.

Again, however, time seems to be on the side of the new varieties. Crosses between them and the local strains often eliminate the less desirable characteristics, and consumer tastes adapt with time. Meanwhile, scores of local rice-research stations are kept informed about these technical problems. New varieties that are more disease-resistant, that require less expensive protection in the form of chemical controls, and that have more desirable cooking and milling properties are being developed all the time.

Economic Constraints

The economic threats to the Green Revolution are more formidable than are the technical ones. Scarcities of foreign exchange and of farm credit and declining cereal prices are certain to slow the spread of the new seeds.

One of the great ironies of the Green Revolution is that the achievement of self-sufficiency in food may create a more serious foreign-exchange crisis than would continued dependence on food aid from abroad. Because food aid comes in kind and not in money, the savings in American food aid, for example, cannot be used to buy the increased amounts of fertilizer and other farm inputs needed to use the seeds effectively.

For example, Pakistan has been receiving about $150 million a year in wheat imports under the American food-aid programs. To replace this food aid, Pakistan will have to spend perhaps $40 million a year on imports of fertilizer and other farm inputs. This money initially must come out of other aid funds or out of Pakistant's growing but still meager foreign-exchange earnings.

There is no functioning mechanism within the United States government for transferring savings in food aid to increased aid in other forms so that at least a portion of the budget savings realized from reductions in the food-aid program could be shifted to finance the import of fertilizer and other items needed to sustain the agricultural revolution in aid-receiving countries. The two forms of aid are the responsibilities of separate Congressional committees: food aid is the province of the agricultural committees; fertilizer and other forms of aid, of the foreign-affairs committees.

Some countries, such as oil-rich Iran, have the money with which to buy the inputs needed for self-sufficiency in food.

But many poor countries have no such prospect. They cannot meet the heavy demands for foreign exchange, needed particularly to buy fertilizer raw materials, which self-sufficiency in food will require in the years immediately ahead.

Poor countries are, however, building fertilizer plants, but these, too, require capital. Once the plants are in operation, they will reduce, but not eliminate, the foreign-exchange demand. Only the United States and the Soviet Union are fortunate enough to have within their boundaries commercial deposits of all the raw materials needed for a modern fertilizer industry—phosphate rock, potash, sulphur and petroleum or natural gas. Most countries must import at least a portion of their fertilizer raw materials, but some, such as India and Thailand, must import nearly all.

As we saw in Chapter 7, technology is changing within the fertilizer industry as it is within agriculture itself; the long-term outlook for fertilizer prices is definitely downward. But this fact is not going to help the poor countries much in their drive for self-sufficiency in food unless the foreign-exchange gap can somehow be bridged. With little land left to bring into cultivation, there is no real alternative to intensifying production on existing land, and that means more capital expenditures for fertilizer. Here again, the course of the Green Revolution will depend importantly on what the rich countries do. Their aid policies will quite directly determine the speed with which the drive toward self-sufficiency in food proceeds.

CREDIT FOR SMALL FARMERS

The supply of farm credit in the poor countries is another important factor in the future of the Green Revolution. The problem is analogous to that in marketing; traditional sources of credit, principally local money lenders, quickly become inadequate as agriculture begins to modernize and purchased inputs become essential. There are no easy ways to create new institutions and sharply expand the supply of credit to millions of small farmers. If traditional sources of credit are typically expensive, it is in part because of the small size of loans needed by the masses of borrowers.

Basically, the problem is to persuade institutional lenders, such as commercial banks, to move into the countryside on a large scale. In some countries this is beginning to happen. Moroccan farmers who are participating in an accelerated wheat-production program are receiving credit free of interest. Much of the money for this comes out of a revolving credit fund, established in part with the local currency proceeds of American food aid.

The Philippines faces special problems: a majority of its farmers are tenants on small holdings who lack collateral for bank loans because they have no title to the land they work. To cope with the situation, an Agricultural Guarantee Loan Fund was established in the Central Bank. Money from the fund, together with insurance against losses on loans, is distributed through 179 widely separated private rural banks, which in turn relend to tenant farmers without the usual collateral requirements and at reasonable interest rates. It was largely in this manner that the farm inputs for the new rice varieties were financed in the Philippines.

In general, production breakthroughs are increasing the number of farmers who are depositors in commercial banks and who therefore are capable of financing their own purchases of production inputs. Typically, of course, it is the larger farmers who are most ready and able to adopt the new technologies and enter the market. This movement has been accelerated by the exceedingly favorable farm prices of the past few years.

However, an inadequate supply of credit is still preventing hundreds of thousands of farmers, particularly small holders, from adopting the new technologies. Montague Yudelman has concluded from his intensive studies of agriculture in

Latin America [1] that one way to resolve this problem may be for governments to subsidize interest rates in ways that encourage commercial banks and other institutional lenders to expand into rural areas. He suggests that bankers who require a 20-per-cent interest rate on small agricultural loans might be responsive to an 8-per-cent subsidy, thus reducing the rate farmers pay to 12 per cent. This would enable an $8-million government subsidy to increase the flow of credit by $100 million. In the inflation-prone economies of the poor countries, it is always difficult to prevent such innovations from simply evaporating in price increases, but in view of its effect on the number participating in the Green Revolution, this kind of device deserves consideration.

PRICES AND INCENTIVES

The paramount threat to the Green Revolution is increasingly the availability of markets rather than production technology. The governments of the poor countries, with their pathetically inadequate resources, face the dilemma of maintaining a minimum cereal price high enough to encourage efficient farmers to invest in the new technologies, but not so high as to produce unmarketable surpluses.

Expanding production of wheat and rice in several Asian countries, following years of scarcity, is already pushing prices downward. In some countries, prices are resting at the government support level. The Philippine Rice and Corn Production Coordinating Council, the price-supporting agency, used up so much of its funds buying rice at high prices in 1968 that it had only limited funds with which to support the 1969 crop. The Council's rice represents the first exportable surplus from the Philippines in almost fifty years, but with the continuing decline in world prices, it can now be exported

[1] M. Yudelman, *Agricultural Development in Latin America: Current Status and Prospects*, Washington, D.C.: Inter-American Development Bank, 1966, Appendix II.

only at a substantial loss. Meanwhile, should the government not have the resources to maintain the announced support price in 1969, agricultural progress in the Philippines could be set back seriously.

This could become a pattern in many countries, as cereal production continues to surge ahead. Several countries now in a position to export or fast approaching that position are facing grave problems because internal prices are higher than the world market price. Included in this group in addition to the Philippines are Mexico (wheat), Kenya (corn), and Pakistan (wheat).

From the point of view of the rich countries, with their modern agricultural economies either dependent on exports, as is true of the United States, or built on protection, as in Western Europe and Japan, the threat of a serious decline in world cereal prices already looms large. They are beginning to realize that they must start planning now for a very different global pattern of agricultural production during the 1970's than that which existed in the 1960's.

The rich countries cannot alone maintain the momentum of the Green Revolution, but unless they act wisely they can retard the agricultural progress which they themselves have helped to make possible. Whether they act effectively will depend upon a much deeper understanding of how the second-generation problems of this revolution relate to the fundamental issues of our time, such as overpopulation, hunger, poverty, excessive urbanization, and unemployment.

IV

Solving Urban Problems
in the Countryside

12

The New Seeds and the Cities

Since the Industrial Revolution, the most enduring social phenomenon everywhere has been the steady movement of population from the farm to the city. This historic trek has created the stark possibility that many great cities may become human trash heaps, the very opposite of the centers of civilization envisoned by the Greek philosophers.

Whether en route to Newark, New Jersey, or Calcutta, India, hundreds of millions have voted with their feet for almost any alternative to remaining in the countryside. In Newark they crowd the ghettos; in Calcutta a hundred thousand or so have become permanent inhabitants of the sidewalks. Now, the new seeds offer at least a possibility of slowing down the flow from countryside to city in the poor regions of the world, where the problems of "urbanization" are currently so pressing and potentially so explosive. But, ironically, if the new technologies are mismanaged, they can displace rural populations, driving them into the cities.

Many current urban problems, whether in Newark or Calcutta, have their roots in the technological changes that have taken place in the countryside. The black migrant to Newark was driven out of the South by the mechanical cotton picker. After two centuries, one of the most important original reasons for bringing blacks to the United States from Africa—to pick cotton—suddenly disappeared. For many there was no alternative to migration to the urban areas of the North, if

101

only to take advantage of better social services or bigger welfare checks.

A different kind of technological innovation drove millions
from the rural areas of West Bengal into Calcutta. Two decades of exploding population growth, the result of successful
malaria-eradication projects and other modern medical advances, increased the pressure of people on the land in Bengal
to the point where literally millions of Bengalis had neither
land nor the prospect of enough employment in the countryside to ward off starvation. Desperation led them to the city.

The plight of the cities is far worse in the poor countries
than in the United States. Here, at least, there has been some
reverse trek from the inner cities to the suburbs; the density
of the ghettos in big cities like New York is not greater and
may even be somewhat less than it was a generation ago. But
there is no such hope of escape from Calcutta or Bombay or
Bogota.

RURAL POPULATION TRENDS

Despite migration to the cities, rural populations are expanding in virtually all poor countries and are projected to do
so for years, if not decades, to come. The rural population is so
large and its increase so rapid that its growth more than com-
pensates for the loss to urban migration. In the crowded country of India, a landless population has grown up in the
countryside that is larger than the total population of Great
Britain. These rootless people cannot even enjoy the status of
tenant farmers but exist as an impoverished force of seasonally
unemployed farm labor.

There are exceptions to this trend, such as Taiwan, Turkey,
and Israel. Taiwan's economy, which probably grew faster
during the 'sixties than any other except Japan's, is nearing
the point where the prospect of industrial and commerical employment is drawing enough people off the land to bring
about a reduction in the rural population. Turkey's farm-

labor force appears to have peaked in the late 1960's, at an uncommonly early stage of development. This appears to be due in part to the migration of several hundred thousand Turkish workers to Europe, especially Western Germany, to work in industry. Israel's farm-labor force, which grew rapidly in the early years after the partition of Palestine as a result of natural increase and immigration, also seems to have peaked. The importation of large amounts of investment capital made rapid industrial expansion possible and with it a rapid increase in non-farm employment opportunities.

But these are the exceptions. The world's population remains predominantly rural; more than half of its people live in rural Asia, Africa, and Latin America. For years to come, this large and growing group must make its living in agriculture. The resources to create jobs elsewhere in the economy can accommodate only a small share of the increase in rural population. Properly managed, the new technologies can create farm employment and make rural life otherwise more attractive.

THE NEW SEEDS AND FARM LABOR

Wherever data are available, they indicate that the new seeds require more labor than the traditional ones they replace. Farmers who wish to realize the genetic potential of the high-yielding seeds must prepare seedbeds more thoroughly, apply fertilizer more frequently, weed more carefully, and use pesticides. All these operations require additional labor.

In northern India and West Pakistan, where the high-yielding wheats are catching on quickly, seasonal labor shortages have been aggravated, forcing rural wages during harvest above the wages prevailing in the larger cities. A survey cited in an AID report from New Delhi in 1969 showed that the cash outlays for hired labor needed to produce the new rices are roughly double the outlays required for local rices. A scattering of data from several countries indicates that total labor requirements, both family and hired labor, are from 10 per cent to as much as 60 per cent greater with the new seeds, depending on local growing conditions and labor costs.

A report from the AID mission in New Delhi, addressed to the effect of the new wheats on employment, concludes:

> The Green Revolution has definitely been employment-creating. In the Punjab [state in northern India] there have been serious labor shortages during the April–June period when wheat is harvested, threshed, marketed and the summer crop is sown. Non-agricultural wage rates have risen as high as $2.00–$3.25 per day. Agricultural labor rates have also risen. Mechanization is increasing rapidly, largely because of the labor shortages.

This conclusion is borne out by experience in such countries as Taiwan and Japan, where, as agriculture modernized, labor requirements increased. Japanese and Taiwanese farmers now invest about 170 man-days in the production and harvesting of an acre of rice, as compared with 125 man-days in India and 100 in the Philippines. But while more labor is required per acre in Japan and Taiwan, less labor is required per ton of grain. Available data suggest that a similar situation obtains in Turkey, India and Pakistan, where labor used per ton of the new cereals averages perhaps 20 per cent less than with traditional varieties.

The Effect of Mechanization

As wages rise, and as the new seeds make agriculture more profitable, mechanization becomes increasingly attractive. Perhaps the most immediate issue of the agricultural revolution is whether mechanization will come so fast as to displace large numbers of farm laborers and thereby measurably worsen an already serious social problem.

As we saw in Chapter 9, there are bound to be serious conflicts over the division of benefits created by the new seeds between landowners and tenants, and between the country-side and the cities. If mechanization proceeds so rapidly that more millions are added to the army of unemployed in the rural areas and in the cities, the agricultural revolution could become a curse rather than a blessing.

But with the new seeds, selective mechanization can create jobs. Irrigation is a case in point. Traditional methods of irrigation, using human or animal power, often do not supply enough water to meet minimum needs. More important, phenomenal savings occur when mechanized water pumping is introduced. One study of pumping costs in India found that it costs 495 rupees to pump 10 acre-inches of water by hand, assuming a 40-foot lift. With draft animals powering a Persian wheel, the cost drops to 345 rupees, but the really startling gain comes with the use of a diesel engine; the cost then drops to 60 rupees.[1]

As more water becomes available and production is boosted, more labor is required for land preparation, planting, fertilizing, weeding, harvesting, and threshing. When multiple cropping becomes possible, labor requirements may double or even treble, with the number of crops.

Crop production consists of a sequence of operations distributed throughout the year. Where only human labor is available, labor scarcity at planting and harvesting times can be the principal factor limiting food production. Mechanization of selected operations can overcome labor shortages during peak periods, raising the level of farm activity throughout the year. The conventional wisdom that farm mechanization is labor-displacing and therefore undesirable in countries with large numbers of unemployed no longer holds. Selective mechanization can be employment-creating.

Once the availability of water and fertilizer permits con-

---

[1] John S. Balis, *An Analysis of Performance and Costs of Irrigation Pumps Utilizing Manual, Animal and Engine Power,* New Delhi, India: Agency for International Development, 1968, p. 4.

tinuous year-round cropping, then pressure increases to reduce the time between the ripening of one crop and the planting of the next. Farmers can no longer afford to leave land
idle. Dr. Lyle Schertz, of the U.S. Department of Agriculture,
estimates that a rice farmer in Asia who uses the new varieties
faces a loss of 30 pounds of grain per acre every day his land
lies idle between crops. That is enough to feed a man for a
month. Armed with this knowledge, neither governments nor
farmers can afford to leave land idle. And the more intensive
the use of land, the more jobs that are created.

Taiwan provides good examples of how selective mechanization, combined with intensive land use, creates jobs. There,
some farmers are growing three and four crops a year. Seedbed preparation is hastened by the use of Japanese-style tillers,
comparable to the larger garden tractors used in the United
States. Use of these two-wheeled, four- to ten-horsepower tillers reduces the labor required to prepare the seedbed but
increases the number of crops produced, creating more employment.

Despite the fears of some, farm mechanization need not be
an open invitation to social chaos. But it can be, if the benefits
and costs of only the largest and richest farmers are considered. Farm mechanization can bring social disaster if it is not
selective and if it does not encourage a more intensive use of
labor.

Taiwan, whose farm-labor force is projected to begin declining soon, may find it desirable to mechanize a wide range
of farming operations rather rapidly. India, whose farm-labor
force may continue to grow for decades to come, must be
much more selective in the types of mechanization that are
encouraged.

EMPLOYMENT POTENTIAL OF THE GREEN REVOLUTION

There is no more urgent or difficult task facing policy-
makers in poor countries today than that of fashioning poli-

cies that will encourage enough farm mechanization to sustain the momentum of the Green Revolution but not so much that those who are displaced from the countryside overwhelm the cities. Recent sporadic outbursts of violence in India suggest that the Indian government, for example, has not faced up to this problem.

The solution is to encourage selective mechanization and intensive cropping, both of which create jobs. The Indian government did this when, after 1965, it reoriented its rural electrification policies to give priority to areas with large underground water supplies. Providing electricity in these strategic areas created opportunities for using land and labor that would otherwise be idle. East Pakistan's removal of import duties on low-lift irrigation pumps was similarly well designed. However, these are but small beginnings. A wide range of price, investment, tax, credit, and import policies must be properly orchestrated if the employment potential of the Green Revolution is to be fully realized.

The new seeds and their associated technologies will automatically create what economists call new "backward and forward linkages" with the non-farm economy. Earlier chapters have suggested something of how this works. To sustain rapid growth in farm production, there must be a large and expanding investment in those activities that supply inputs to the farmer and help him to market and process his crop. All these activities are employment-creating. They are integral parts of the process we call industrialization. The Green Revolution destroys once and for all the illusion that agriculture and industry are somehow competitors for exclusive priority in government policy. They have to go forward hand in hand; neither can advance very far alone.

As far as agriculture is concerned, this means that there must be a continually expanding demand for farm products. As long as there is an internal food deficit to produce against, production can expand rather rapidly. But once this is filled, demand will increase rapidly only if export markets are developed. A rise in domestic demand depends upon a rapid and continuing indigenous growth in incomes; a rise in the demand for export depends upon gaining access to the highly protected grain markets of the rich countries, particularly Japan and Western Europe, a problem to which we will return in Chapters 19 and 20.

Neither an adequate growth in incomes nor adequate access to export markets can be achieved by efforts of the poor countries alone. In other words, the employment potential of the agricultural revolution cannot be realized if the poor countries are regarded as closed economies. The infinite possibilities inherent in the Green Revolution, therefore, are just as much the responsibilities of the rich as of the poor countries. We can either stand aside and wring our hands over the possibility of instability and violence as the new seeds spread, or we can try to tilt the balance in favor of a brighter, more hopeful future for all.

Creating employment opportunities for more of the millions who are trying to find a productive place in modern society will probably be the principal challenge of the 1970's, whether we are concerned with those who left the countryside for the ghettos of Newark or for the sidewalks of Calcutta. Each country must analyze its own situation, identifying those activities which, if mechanized, would intensify agricultural production and create additional employment. Governments should then use all available policy instruments to encourage the mechanization of those activities which create jobs, while discouraging mechanization that is largely labor-displacing. Policies governing farm mechanization may have greater influence on the distribution of benefits of the agricultural revolution than policies in any other area.

Because the new seeds promise to increase the food supply markedly, it is possible to view population problems in a new perspective, placing employment ahead of food supply as the major immediate problem. But before we examine this idea (in Chapter 14), there is one further constraint that demands our attention: the prevailing system of land tenure in many of the poor countries.

13

Rising Pressures for Agricultural Reform

One of the puzzling dimensions of the agricultural revolution is why it is progressing so spectacularly in some poor countries but not catching on at all in others. It is true that new wheats and rices are better adapted to some countries than others, but this variability does not begin to explain the glaring contrasts. The Mexican dwarf wheats, for example, are spreading through much of Asia and parts of North Africa but are having little impact in Latin America outside Mexico. Nor are the dwarf rices developed in the Philippines catching on rapidly in Latin America.

In general, the disparities are due to the inability of some governments to create the economic climate required to accommodate a breakthrough in agriculture—more specifically, to their inability to bring about land reform. Even if price incentives are provided, land ownership in many countries is too concentrated within a small segment of the population to permit an effective link between effort and reward for those who work the land. In other cases, the small size of land holdings or the fact that land tenure is determined by archaic customs effectively prevents the introduction of modern technologies.

There are those who take an ideological view of agricultural reform—or agrarian reform, as they usually call it. But a pragmatic view seems more appropriate, given the great promise of the new seeds and their associated technologies.

110

LAND REFORM

Countries that turn in outstanding agricultural perform-ances, whether they are rich or poor, are usually those in which land ownership is widely distributed throughout the rural population. This includes Japan, Taiwan, Mexico, and the United States. Each of the first three reformed its pattern of land ownership during this century. The United States pattern of land ownership, concentrated in a few hands dur-ing the colonial period as a result of large land grants from the Crown to such personages as Lord Baltimore and William Penn, broadened rapidly after Abraham Lincoln signed the Homestead Act into law in 1862. This legislation not only gave free land to those who were willing to homestead but also sharply reduced the supply of rural labor in the East, making the large land grants from the Crown exceedingly costly, if not impossible, to maintain.

It is more than mere happenstance that the Green Revolu-tion took hold first in Mexico and then spread, not to the rest of Latin America, but to Asia. Both Mexico and Taiwan had instituted effective, far-reaching land-reform programs prior to their dramatic advances in agricultural production. This was less true of India and Pakistan, but in these countries land in the countryside had been divided and subdivided for generations as population pressures grew and the availability of new arable lands diminished. In Latin America, however, less than 5 per cent of the population owns 95 per cent of the arable land. Even though land is plentiful, the great bulk of the farm-labor force consists of landless laborers.

Where land ownership is concentrated in a few hands, and especially where this concentration effectively prevents modernization, governments must eventually redistribute land so as to broaden the base of land ownership. Land reform is not an easy task, and its initial effects on agricultural production are sometimes adverse. The unavoidable disruptions associated with the process of redistributing or resettling land are not at first conducive to rapid expansion in production. Many who find themselves owners of land for the first time lack even rudimentary management skills. They are usually heavily dependent on government subsidies and services, and governments in the poor countries can rarely afford to pay the subsidies and supply the services effectively for extended periods.

Yet as agriculture emerges from its traditional subsistence state to modern commercial farming, with the need to purchase inputs and market production surpluses, it becomes progressively more important to ensure that adequate rewards accrue directly to the man who tills the soil. Indeed, it is hard to see how there can be any meaningful modernization of food production in Latin America and Africa south of the Sahara unless land is registered, deeded, and distributed more equitably among those who till it. If land titles in Africa continue to be determined arbitrarily by a chief or headman, there simply will be no basis for investment in the land. If the link between effort and reward in Latin America is weakened because huge tracts of land are owned by absentee landlords or country gentlemen with little interest in commercial farming, millions will continue to abandon the countryside for the impoverished city barrios.

TECHNIQUES OF LAND REFORM

The techniques used to achieve land reform are many and varied. The Kenya government has had notable success in negotiating the registration and deeding of plots in former tribal lands, something the British colonial administrators could not do. In Kenya, land tenure is such as to accommodate the Green Revolution. In general, however, land-reform schemes involve one of two broadly defined courses of action: either expropriating large holdings and subsequently redistributing parcels to formerly landless laborers or tenants, or opening new areas to settlement and giving titles to those who did not previously have land. The latter is politically less painful, but it requires much more capital and is almost always a very slow process.

Whether it involves expropriation or colonization, land reform must be conducted quickly; otherwise the uncertainties associated with any long-term investment in agriculture will discourage the new land owners from making the needed investments or even from occupying the new land. In any case, if reform is not quick, farm production may stagnate or decline, as was the case in Mexico between 1910 and 1940, when the government promoted a piecemeal and hesitant series of reform programs. This may be the situation in Chile today.

Morocco and Mexico have used irrigation policy as a means of distributing land. In both countries, farmers are required to pay part of the cost of local irrigation works provided by the government. In Mexico, farmers with less than 375 acres pay in cash; those with farms of more than 375 acres are required to pay in land. Moroccan farmers with less than 12 acres are exempt from sharing the capital cost of local irrigation projects.

Small Farms and Modern Technologies

The distribution of land ownership among those who work it has a far greater influence on agricultural modernization than does farm size. Farm size, in fact, is not nearly so important as many Western analysts consider it to be. Proof of this is the fact that two of the pacesetters in agricultural development, Japan and Taiwan, have the smallest farms, averaging less than three acres each.

We saw in Chapter 12 that selective mechanization and intensive cropping tend to create jobs when the new seeds are introduced. These decisions favor small farms where family labor, which is essentially free, is an important input. Large farmers, faced with the need to hire numbers of workers to tend intensively cultivated land, might find the wage costs too high to justify use of the new seeds. In fact, when a group of Indian wheat farmers was asked why they were not using the new varieties, about a quarter of them answered that the cost of the additional hired labor that would be needed was too high.

The equalizing factor for the large farmer is mechanization, of course. In fact, the greater the need for capital to buy inputs, the greater the comparative advantage of large farms. Here again, we see the crucial importance of government policies toward the encouragement of mechanization. The large farmer's penchant for mechanization can involve a frightful social cost. The danger inherent in the Green Revolution stems from that threat; the hope stems from the real economies and production increases that now can be realized on small farms with labor-intensive cultivation.

But the choice is not just between big farms and small farms; there are numerous intermediate possibilities that can help to reconcile the competing objectives of higher productivity and a more widespread pattern of land ownership.

Consolidated Farming

A new form of production organization is evolving, apparently independently, in several rice-producing countries. It minimizes the disadvantages of small farm size while permitting farmers to take advantage of many of the benefits of large-scale operations. Known as consolidated or joint farming organizations, these production arrangements involve the consolidation of several small farms into a single large unit for management purposes. They are something of a hybrid, combining some characteristics of a family farm with some of a collective. Usually voluntary, they permit farmers to have the best of both worlds, benefitting from the intensity of cultivation associated with small holdings and the economies of scale deriving from larger operations, while preserving the advantages of direct ownership.

These coordinated multifarm units are especially advantageous where farms are small and the proportion of land in bunds (earthen dikes separating small individual rice plots) is high (Taiwan); where effective water control or management is often possible only on a multifarm basis (Malaysia); where fields are so small that mechanization of certain operations is not feasible; where a large number of adjacent farms produce the same crop during the same season (Thailand); and where farm labor is becoming scarce as a result of rapid industrial development (Taiwan), a reduced rate of population growth, or some combination of the two (Japan).

In Taiwan, the new production organizations permit individual farmers to retain title to their land and divide the harvest on a prorated basis, while coordinating such farming operations as planting, irrigating, and pest control. Efforts to develop joint farming operations thus far have been concentrated in rice-growing areas, where production has risen 10–25 per cent in the consolidated farms. The gains derive from planting the field border areas previously occupied by bunds as well as from better water control and management.

Thus far in Taiwan, 7,000 acres of land in eight locations, with a minimum of 750 acres each, have been consolidated into single production units. The bunds have been eliminated, thus permitting the combination of numerous small plots into a single large field with unified water management and control and uniform planting dates. Some 550 smaller joint projects, averaging 40 acres of rice land each, are also in operation. A similar effort for field crops is just beginning. The goal of the Taiwan government is to have 250,000 acres— one tenth of the cropland—in joint farming operations by 1972.

A similar voluntary effort in Thailand includes 167 blocks of consolidated farms and a total of 29,000 acres. With rice output on these blocks up by 60 per cent, the consolidated area is expected to expand steadily.

Malaysia is planning to experiment with group production of several crops, including rice, various fruits, coconuts, corn, and cassava, wherever transport, drainage, and irrigation facilities make this practical. Efforts of a similar nature are under way in Japan, specifically designed to encourage mechanization and to conserve scarce rural labor.

How far this pattern in cooperative relations will progress is conjectural at this point. Prospective production gains of 10–60 per cent provide strong incentive for farmers to integrate their efforts into larger management units. But the potential area that will benefit from such integration may be limited by the availability of the management skills needed to direct such an operation.

SERVICING SMALL FARMS

Farm consolidation seems to have special advantages in rice-growing areas where water control is a significant problem. In other situations and with other crops, a better strategy for overcoming the disadvantages of small farms might involve improving the package of credit, marketing, and extension services. There would seem to be a good case, too, for developing custom-hire services to provide small farmers with the benefits of farm mechanization.

Indian farmers whose holdings are less than the optimal size for one team of bullocks often maintain a team anyway, paying a high price for the limited use they make of it. Access to custom-hire services would permit the small holder to gain some of the benefits from mechanization and perhaps to dispense entirely with his bullocks. Similarly, in Thailand, where farmers maintain a team of water buffalo solely for preparing the rice seedbed once a year, hiring someone with a tractor to plow the rice fields would enable them to dispense with their buffalo and realize substantial savings. Prior to custom plow-ing a small farmer had no choice but to maintain his own team of buffalo.

Custom-hire services are one of the most effective means of bridging the gap between large-scale modern farms and small traditional ones. They also enable peasant farmers to overcome labor shortages at the peak periods of land preparation and harvesting. Governments can either encourage private entrepreneurs to establish custom-hire tractor services or provide such services themselves. However, where governments have undertaken to supply these services, the record has been uniformly disappointing. An AID study in Nigeria indicates that the tractor-hire services provided by the Nigerian Ministry of Agriculture cost taxpayers $700 a year for each tractor. In Tanzania a similar effort was so costly and inefficient that it was eventually abandoned and the equipment sold at auction to private entrepreneurs.

These failures seem to have resulted from the government's lack of flexibility in operating these services, and from a lack of incentive to provide them efficiently. Governments have an interest in seeing that custom-hire services are available to small farmers, but their objectives are more likely to be attained if private entrepreneurs provide the service.

The new seeds make agricultural reform even more crucial, while at the same time offering new hope that reform will come in an orderly way. It can no longer be doubted that changes in the pattern of land ownership and tenure in many parts of the world, especially Latin America and sub-Saharan Africa, must come if the new technologies are to take root there. On the other hand, the great promise of the new seeds should make it possible to achieve reform without total destruction of the existing social order.

V

Population, Employment, and Hunger

14

Redefining the Population Problem

When Thomas Malthus published his gloomy treatise in 1798, he defined the population problem primarily in terms of food supplies and the threat of famine. Ever since, the threat of overpopulation has been perceived largely in his terms. In the 1960's, when national and international leaders were preoccupied with food scarcities in the poor countries, the population problem was regarded as virtually synonymous with the food-population problem. The two terms were often used interchangeably.

But as we enter the 1970's we are faced with a need to re-define the population problem. After nearly two centuries, it is time to move beyond our legacy from Malthus.

Two independent phenomena, both bearing directly on the population issue, are forcing us to change our conception of it. The first is the agricultural breakthrough in the poor countries. Although this is by no means a solution to the population problem, it is diminishing the prospects of famine in the near future and buying time—perhaps an additional fifteen years—in which to develop the technologies, the will, and the strategies to stabilize global population growth.

While the threat of famine is diminishing, the number of young people entering labor markets is rising very rapidly. This is the second phenomenon. The population explosion began in most poor countries fifteen or twenty years ago and

121

resulted in an almost immediate demand for additional food. But, since babies do not require employment, there is a grace period of fifteen or twenty years on the job front that does not exist for food. As we enter the 'seventies we approach the end of this grace period. The food-population problem of the 'sixties is becoming the employment-population problem of the 'seventies. Feeding the increased numbers of people will not be easy, but it is likely to prove much more manageable than providing jobs.

THE EMPLOYMENT-POPULATION EQUATION

With more and more young people entering the job market, the day of reckoning with the explosion in population growth has arrived. In some countries the number of young people coming of employment age will nearly double in a matter of years. If these millions of young people are not able to find jobs, the "labor force explosion" could pose an even greater threat to peace and stability than did the threat of famine in the 'sixties.

As we saw in Chapter 12, the Green Revolution can be a tremendous source of additional jobs. Selective mechanization coupled with intensive cultivation can provide millions of new farm jobs. Even more jobs will be created if the poor countries are admitted into competition for the agricultural markets of the rich countries. Still more will be created as industries grow up to provide the farmer with the new inputs he needs to process and market his products. Finally, as the farmer becomes an ever-better customer for the products of industry, industry will need to expand to meet his demands.

But just as mechanical power can be substituted for man-power on the farm, at great social cost, so machines can be substituted for men throughout the industrial sector, with unfortunate effects. The labor force explosion demands that virtually all governments in the poor countries give priority to job creation in the 'seventies equal to that finally accorded to food production in the 'sixties.

Nor is this a problem for governments only. The International Labor Organization, in a document on *The World Employment Program* that helped it earn the Nobel Peace Prize in 1969, argues eloquently that employment creation should be the objective of the international development-assistance effort of the 'seventies. Certainly the hopes of those who are concerned with the population problem will rest on the ability of society to create vast numbers of new jobs.

We are late in coming to this realization. Even the concepts of employment and unemployment in poor, transitional societies remain vague. In all poor countries, the bulk of the population still follows traditional pursuits that keep people in society but out of the labor force as we know it. Modern economic activity exists side by side with traditional or subsistence activities, with all manner of gradations in between. That human energy is not put to productive use, as economists apply the term, is not necessarily a source of discontent in traditional societies. To the contrary, a distinctive feature of this type of society is that it gives its members a sense of place and belonging regardless of their "productivity." But in today's technical society, there is an urgency to the labor-force explosion that derives from the fact that millions of young people are breaking away from the shelter of traditional society to seek a place in modern life.

The ILO hopes to develop some useful ways to quantify the employment problem in poor countries—in the words of Director General David Morse, to "define concrete and realistic employment objectives for economic development policies." This is a complex research task; it is very difficult, given our current knowledge, to think of devising useful indices of unemployment for a country like India that are modeled on the indices used in rich countries.

Despite the difficulty of defining precisely what constitutes the labor force, the fact remains that there are a great many people in the poor countries whose labor potential is under-utilized by any standard. Large numbers, especially in the rural areas, are only bystanders in the process of economic growth. The magnitude of the future problem is suggested by Figure 3, which shows the age structure of populations in selected geographic regions. The pyramid-shaped forms for South Asia and Latin America, contrasting sharply with the industrial regions, indicate dramatic, continuing increases in the numbers of young people entering the job market.

What this means for rural areas can be illustrated by the case of West Pakistan. Between 1951 and 1961, non-farm employment grew at the rate of 4.5 per cent per year, a rate which, in the postwar period, appears to have been exceeded only in Taiwan.[1] Even if this rate of growth were to continue until 1985, workers in the rural sector would still increase only from 7.4 million (in 1961) to 12.2 million. The situation will be worse in many other poor countries. Hundreds of millions of jobs must be created in the coming decade if the world's poor are to have a chance to improve their lives.

The need to develop new technology to create modern *labor-intensive* economic opportunities presents a challenge to economists and planners. We in the rich countries are accustomed to equating modern economic activity with labor-saving economies; in the poor countries we must think in terms of labor-creating economies. The pragmatic need is to encourage as much modern, labor-intensive economic activity as can be produced using the combined resources of the poor and the rich countries.

Capital and other resources from the rich countries can be transferred through government or private channels to create jobs for the burgeoning numbers of young people in the poor

[1] B. F. Johnston, *Agriculture and Economic Development: The Relevance of the Japanese Experience,* Stanford, Calif.: Food Research Institute Studies, Vol. 6, 1966, p. 274.

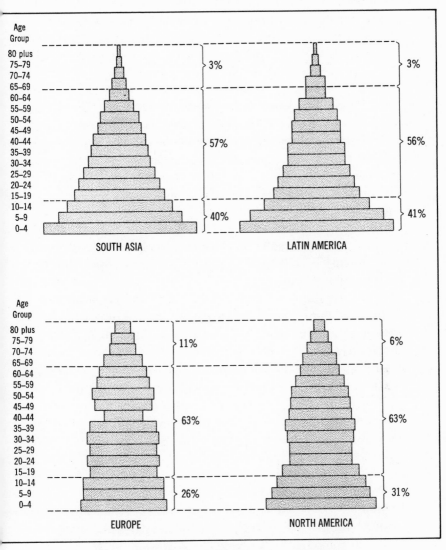

Figure 3. AGE STRUCTURE OF POPULATION IN SELECTED REGIONS
(Width of bars indicates proportion of total population in age group.)

countries. But the prospective transfers of public resources cannot begin to create the necessary numbers of jobs. If the poor countries are to provide jobs for their young people, they must turn to the private sector for new sources of capital and expanded participation by the multinational corporations.

In the second half of the twentieth century, the multinational corporation has demonstrated its capacity to create economic opportunities in poor countries. There is no larger pool of risk capital, managerial talent, and technical knowledge. Most important, the goal of agricultural modernization, to which more and more countries that use the new seeds are subscribing, cannot be achieved unless the poor countries become much more active participants in the international markets, first for cereals and other farm products, and later for labor-intensive industrial exports. Insofar as the multinational corporation brings with it an international marketing network for the products of the poor countries, it becomes indispensable to them. No other institution is even remotely comparable in its capacity to create the jobs they need so desperately.

In dealing with the population problem in the years ahead, we must avoid repeating the errors of the past by not focusing exclusively on one dimension of the problem, whether employment or food. Although employment looms large for the immediate future, it is far from the only one that must be considered.

THE ECOLOGY OF POPULATION GROWTH

Man, in his search for food, is altering his environment at an accelerating pace. In the poor countries particularly, efforts to produce food are destroying the environment. Rich countries have had this experience, too, but the ecological implications of man's quest for food are still only beginning to be understood.

As population grows, an ever-expanding area is cleared of natural cover as the land is used for cultivation. As a result of rising needs for fuel for heat and cooking, the forests are cut far in excess of natural replenishment. The areas thus stripped of forest include the Indian subcontinent, where much of the population must now use cow dung for fuel. Livestock populations tend to increase along with human population, and forage needs for cattle now far exceed replenishment in many poor countries, denuding the countryside of grass cover.

As population pressure builds, not only is more land brought under the plow, but the land remaining is less suited to cultivation. Once valleys are filled, farmers begin to move up hillsides, creating serious soil-erosion problems. As the natural cover that retards runoff is reduced and soil structure deteriorates, floods and droughts become more severe.

Denudation of the countryside and the resulting soil erosion is widespread in much of the developing world. The relationship between man and the land from which he derives his subsistence has become very unstable in large portions of India, particularly in the north and west, and in parts of Pakistan, the Middle East, North Africa, and Central America. Millions of acres of crop land are so severely eroded that they are being abandoned. Many of the displaced farmers and their families are moving to urban areas, swelling the slums.

In addition to destroying soils, severe erosion can impair and eventually destroy irrigation systems as well. The overcutting of forests in Java, an island of 70 million people, causes silting of the irrigation canals and steadily reduces the capacity of existing irrigation systems. Each year the damage from floods, droughts, and erosion becomes more severe.

West Pakistan provides an unfortunate example of the cost of denudation of the countryside. The recently completed

Mangla Reservoir, in the foothills of the Himalayas, cost $600 million dollars to construct. Its life expectancy is currently estimated at less than 50 years, only half the span anticipated in the feasibility study which justified its construction. The Mangla watershed is eroding rapidly as Pakistan's fast-growing human and livestock population bares the countryside. Gullies cutting through the fertile countryside within a half hour's drive of Rawalpindi are so deep that they have become minor tourist attractions.

If man presses nature too hard, the results can be disastrous. The "dustbowl" years of the 1930's offer an example very close to home. Only after some 20 million acres of crop land were set aside for fallow each year and after thousands of miles of windbreaks were planted was a reasonably stable situation re-established in the southern Great Plains. The United States was lucky to have the resources necessary to correct the mistakes man had made, particularly the ability to withdraw large areas of land from cultivation each year. These options are not readily available to the poor countries.

The pressure of population not only causes man to move onto marginal land but also forces him to intensify agricultural production. This in turn involves the use of fertilizer and pesticides, both of which can seriously pollute the environment. Among pesticides, the chlorinated hydrocarbons, such as DDT and dieldrin, pose a serious threat in that they are both toxic and break down slowly or not at all. Thus the amount in the environment keeps building, reaching damaging concentrations in some situations.

DDT tends to concentrate in the predatory forms of life, including man. Such concentration adversely affects the reproductive capacities of certain birds, such as eagles and hawks, and some types of fish. Its precise effect on human life at current levels of concentration in the environment is not known.

Suffice it to say that biologists and medical experts are

worried about the potentially harmful effects of DDT on man and other forms of life. Some countries (e.g., Sweden, Denmark, and the United States) and some states (Michigan and Wisconsin) have already partially or totally banned its use, at least temporarily, and others are expecting to do so.

Meanwhile USDA researchers are hard at work attempting to develop biological controls. The release of sterilized male insects has succeeded in reducing pest populations in some experimental situations. Breeding disease-resistant plants has eliminated the need for chemical pest controls in others.

The heavy use of fertilizer causes the accumulation of nitrates in bodies of water, which stimulates excessive growth of certain kinds of plant life, upsetting the ecological balance and, in so doing, destroying many if not all species of fish. Perhaps the most tragic example of this is Lake Erie, once one of the world's fine inland lakes.

PROSPECTS OF REDUCING BIRTH RATES

The population problem needs to be redefined, but its essential nature remains: until birth rates are decreased, it will be with us.

The spread of modern medical technology during the 1940's raised the global rate of natural population increase well above 1 per cent. By 1960, it had reached 2 per cent, where it has since stabilized. But perhaps even more serious than the sheer numerical increase—70,000,000 people annually—is the fact that fully four fifths of this number are being added in the poor countries. Birth rates in the aid-recipient countries are now virtually twice those in the rich countries. In Latin America as a whole, the rate of annual increase has reached an incredible 2.9 per cent, which means that the population will double in only 24 years.

Three alternative projections used by United Nations demographers yield anticipated populations of 5.4, 6.1 and 7.0 billions by the end of the century. World population is currently growing slightly faster than the second of these projections. This means we must prepare for nearly three billion more people between 1970 and 2000, a billion per decade.

The old adage, "the rich get richer and the poor get children," clearly applies in the rich and poor countries. Economic growth in the poor countries is required merely to provide for population increase, leaving little scope for improvement in individual welfare. The reverse is true in the rich countries, where populations grow slowly and most economic progress improves individual welfare. Population growth thus turns out to be the principal contributor to the widening gap between rich and poor.

Birth rates in the rich countries are declining steadily from the post-World War II highs. In the two largest industrial countries, the United States and the Soviet Union, birth rates have declined steadily since 1957. Remarkably parallel trends have dropped crude birth rates to 18 per thousand per year in each, resulting in a yearly rate of natural increase of just under 1 per cent. These trends and similar declines in high-income countries in Europe and in Japan, Australia, and Canada are encouraging.

Successful national family-planning efforts in the poor countries are thus far limited to a few smaller ones, all in East Asia: Taiwan, South Korea, and Hong Kong. If recent trends continue, the peak rates of population growth experienced in these countries should be cut in half by 1975.

In Singapore, a city-state of about two million, population grew at an average of more than 3 per cent a year between 1957 and 1965. Then, the dynamic and energetic Prime Minister, Le Kwan Yew, threw his weight behind an intensive program to promote family planning. The Singapore telephone book today lists 28 family-planning clinics that are advertised as being open 24 hours a day, seven days a week. Virtually all mothers in Singapore have at least one baby at a single large urban hospital, making it easy to reach them with family-planning information and contraceptives. Population growth in Singapore was expected to drop below 2 per cent in 1969, one of the most rapid declines any city of this size ever experienced in peacetime.

But these success stories have occurred in only a few places in the less-developed world. Major deceleration in world population growth awaits a significant reduction in births in India and Pakistan, which together contain nearly 700 million people. (Mainland China should also be included, of course, but reliable statistics from that vast country are hard to come by.) The target of India's family planners is that the population, now approaching 550 million, might be stabilized at 750 million. That would involve reducing today's 2.5 per cent annual growth to about 2 per cent in 1975, and to zero by 1985! Put another way, it requires reducing a birth rate of 41 per thousand to 11 per thousand.

The Indian program attempts to popularize all types of contraceptives. Raising the legal age of marriage, legalized abortions, and even compulsory sterilization for those with three or more children are all being advocated seriously.

An India of 750 millions, of course, will not be free of population pressure. The consequences of crowding three quarters of a billion poverty-stricken people into an area the size of the United States east of the Mississippi are certainly not going to be easy to contend with.

Considering the fantastically high economic returns that can be expected from successful investments in family planning, much greater efforts are justified. The Ford Foundation estimates that worldwide research expenditures on fertility control, currently $25 to $30 million a year, should be increased five- or sixfold. The argument is convincing; until medical researchers find a new contraceptive technology, it will be difficult to achieve a widespread reduction in population growth rates in low-income countries. The major sponsors of contraceptive research today are the Rockefeller and Ford Foundations, the National Institute of Health, the U.S. Agency for International Development, and the Swedish government. Considering the economic and social dividends at stake, a strong case can be made for a much larger contribution by international agencies which thus far have failed to come to grips with the problem. It would be a major tragedy if the time bought by the Green Revolution were wasted only because the relatively modest sums needed were not forthcoming.

THE GREEN REVOLUTION AND FAMILY PLANNING

Breakthroughs in food production and the prospects for effective family-planning efforts in poor countries are not unrelated. In addition to providing time in which to develop new contraceptive techniques, expanded food supplies can have a widespread effect on attitudes toward family planning. The lack of interest in family planning by most couples in these countries is largely due to their feeling that they must bear many children if a few are to survive to adulthood. With less malnutrition, much larger numbers should survive. If assured food supplies are a precondition for the widespread adoption of family planning, as many sociologists believe, then this hurdle is now being crossed in some of the poor countries. Paradoxically, more food could eventually mean fewer people.

Reinforcing this contribution of the Green Revolution to family planning is the likelihood that those who adopt the new seeds will become much more susceptible to change in other areas, including the planning of their families. Once an individual breaks with tradition in agriculture, it becomes easier for him to accept other kinds of change.

The most significant contribution of the Green Revolution to the population debate is likely to be the new context in which that debate will be carried on in the 1970's. The Green

Revolution has, at least temporarily, laid the spectre of famine to rest, permitting an employment crisis of vast proportions to surface in its place. Discussion of the urgency of limiting populating growth must shift its focus from food to jobs.

15

Toward the Eradication of Hunger

The new seeds, as we have seen, are seeds of change, promising to transform the economies of the poor countries, politicize the countryside, and alter the social order. But the new seeds imply something else for humanity, something of paramount importance: they invite mankind to set the goal of eliminating hunger from this planet.

Hunger is not a specific condition, like smallpox, for which there is a specific cure. Measuring hunger statistically is still a very rough art. Yet chronic hunger is one of the most tragic of all human conditions and one that has plagued man since his beginning. The advent of the new seeds means that in a very few years no society need take hunger for granted, as has always been the custom in most traditional cultures.

What we do know about hunger is that it does not owe its existence to man's inability to produce enough food. In the United States, 50 million acres of crop land have been deliberately withdrawn from production in order to avoid glutting the world market with grains it cannot absorb. As the new seeds spread, hunger will become less and less a problem of aggregate production capacity, even in the poor countries themselves.

We know now that hunger is inextricably linked with abject poverty. Its eradication depends less on encouraging new production than on expanding employment opportunities and raising incomes among the impoverished. The new seeds, because they promise both lower food costs and higher incomes, are making this relationship more obvious and thereby are making it more and more difficult not to accept the eradication of hunger for most of mankind as a practical, achievable goal during the decade of the 'seventies.

In addition to the existing excess global capacity, the future is likely to see the anomaly of food surpluses, in the economist's sense of there being more food than the market will readily absorb, existing side by side with widespread hunger in many poor countries. How to use food as a form of capital to create jobs poses a question to which economists must direct their attention. Both AID and FAO have some experience in doing this, but only on a limited scale relative to prospective needs.

THE ANATOMY OF HUNGER

In Zambia, in Africa, 260 of every thousand babies born are dead before their first birthday. In India and Pakistan the ratio is 140 of every thousand; in Colombia it is 82. Many more die before they reach school age; others, during the early school years.

Where death certificates are issued for preschool infants in the poor countries, death is generally attributed to measles, pneumonia, dysentery, or some other disease. In fact, these children are more likely to be the victims of malnutrition. A severely malnourished infant or child with low resistance can die of the most minor ailments. Paul Ehrlich, an ecologist at Stanford, has suggested that all deaths that would not have occurred given adequate nutrition should be attributed to malnutrition. If this could be done with reasonable accuracy, it would bring the suffering and social cost of malnutrition into much sharper focus.

Hunger and malnutrition can be described statistically, but statistics alone have little meaning for most of us. The fact that half or two thirds of the world's people are hungry or malnourished is difficult to comprehend. It does not move us to action. But hunger is meaningful when it is personalized, as in the following account of hunger in Colombia by Frank Byrnes:

Nine-year-old Ana Ruth did not know why her aunt had left her in the hospital. Her younger brother had died at home just two weeks before, and now, when the doctors and nurses came to talk to her, she asked what was going to happen to her. Too young to understand fully the prospect of dying, Ana Ruth was afraid that in some way she would have to part with the new sneakers, dark blue canvas with white rubber soles, that a doctor had given her. So she wore them day and night, lying in her hospital bed, and a sympathetic staff let her, for there is no getting used to watching children die.

Most children in the developing world suffer at one time or another from malnutrition, particularly from protein deficiencies in their early years. The advanced symptoms are easily recognizable: bellies become bloated, legs swell up like balloons, and hair turns reddish-blond and becomes brittle.

Ana Ruth did not die. When her aunt, already overburdened with caring for her own five children, decided to let the University of Valle's hospital worry about the little orphan girl's final care and burial, attendants rushed her to the Metabolic Unit, where Dr. Alberto G. Pradilla and his staff took over. Her condition was critical. She was suffering not only from serious protein deficiency, the disease called *kwashiorkor,* but also from pneumonia, which frequently occurs in victims of malnutrition. As they treated Ana Ruth for pneumonia, doctors also placed her on a minimum-level protein diet, watching carefully the sodium-potassium balance in her system so as to avoid the risk of sudden death from additional strain on the heart.

Ana Ruth responded rapidly. She lost over two pounds of water a day for three consecutive days, and the bloating and swelling abated. Once she was on a recovery diet, her abnormal hair fell out, and her head began to sprout a fuzz promising a luxuriant growth of silky black hair.[1]

Perhaps the most careful global assessment of the incidence of hunger is that in the United States Department of Agriculture's World Food Budget. This analysis divides countries into two groups, the diet-adequate and the diet-inadequate, on the basis of a minimum caloric intake. In 1960 an estimated 1.9 billion lived in countries where the average intake was below the recommended minimum; the daily food-energy deficit averaged 300 calories per person. For some, of course, the gap was far wider. Although there was little change in diets between 1960, when the Food Budget calculations were made, and 1967, preliminary information suggests modest improvements in several poor countries since 1968.

Caloric intake, though a good quantitative indicator of food intake, is not a good indicator of diet quality. For this purpose, protein intake is much more satisfactory. Most of the 1.9 billion who don't get enough calories also suffer from protein deficiencies. Such was the case with Ana Ruth and, very probably, her younger brother, who died two weeks prior to her admission to the hospital. The problem is not just a lack of protein *per se* but a lack of protein of high quality such as is available in animal products or legumes (peas, beans, soybeans, etc.). In many countries the most pressing need is for high-quality protein, and science is rising to this challenge in some very interesting ways.

Many of those who live in perpetual hunger do not die at Ana Ruth's age. Examples of the suffering they endure, however, are legion. It is estimated that there are four million people in India who are totally blind and possibly three times as many who are partially blind, largely owing to Vitamin A

[1] Frances C. Byrnes, "A Matter of Life and Death," *Rockefeller Foundation Quarterly*, 3, 1964, p. 4.

deficiencies. Perhaps one third of the Indian mothers who die in childbirth die because of iron-deficiency anemia.

It seems callous even to try to measure the cost to society of such suffering—of listlessness and sickness, of death so commonplace that fathers and mothers feel that they must have many children simply to ensure that enough will survive to care for them in their old age. Many medical experts doubt that there can be effective curbs on population growth until nutritional standards are raised.

The effect of low levels of food-energy intake on the productivity of labor is easy to see. American construction firms operating in developing countries and employing local labor often find that they get high returns in worker output by investing in a good company cafeteria that serves employees three meals a day. But the scope of this problem is perhaps better illustrated by events during the summer of 1968, when India held its Olympic trials in New Delhi to select a track and field team to go to Mexico City in the fall. Although it had a population of 535 million to draw from, India failed to qualify a single athlete in any of the 32 track and field events. Not one of the contestants could meet the minimum Olympic qualifying standards. Outdated training techniques and a lack of public support were partly responsible, but undernourishment of most of the population certainly contributed to this poor showing.

Although the relationship between diet and physical performance is well known, the parallel relationship between nutrition and mental performance has only recently been demonstrated. Protein shortages in the early years of life impair development of the brain and central nervous system, permanently reducing learning capacity. Furthermore, this damage is irreversible. Protein shortages today are depreciating the stock of human resources for at least a generation to come. And no amount of investment in education can correct this damage.

INCOME AND HUNGER

Many promising ways of solving the huge problem of hunger have been suggested, but most authorities now agree that malnutrition is inseparable from poverty itself. Even in the United States, where there is poverty there is often hunger, too. In the poor countries of the world the connection is impossible to ignore. The World Food Budget shows that the 1.1 billions living in adequately fed countries in 1960 had an average yearly income of $1,070 per person; the 1.9 billions in malnourished countries had an average income of $97. The surest way to improve nutrition is to raise incomes. Diets improve most rapidly where per-capita incomes are growing fastest.

The agricultural revolution not only produces more food; it is also injecting vigor into the economies of the poor countries. These two of course are interrelated. As the income of farmers is raised, they retain more of the food they produce for home consumption and also buy more goods and services, thus providing more employment and higher incomes for the non-farm population. This in turn expands demand for the increased food production. The effect of the agricultural revolution on cereal production per person is shown in Table 8. In Mexico, eight consecutive record harvests add up to some impressive gains, raising per-capita cereal output far above the annual 400-pound level of grain, or grain equivalent in other starchy foods, required for direct consumption. Since the grain available for conversion into animal protein more than doubled during the 'sixties, Mexico now has a solid resource base from which to develop a modern poultry and livestock industry.

This process is just beginning in Asia, but we can anticipate advances in at least some countries to match the Mexican performance. The breakthrough in cereal production in Asia is occurring first in wheat, as illustrated by the striking gains in both Pakistan and India. In these two countries, it is only beginning in rice, the number-one staple, and other cereals. The countries achieving the greatest advances in rice production per person thus far are Ceylon, Malaysia, and the Philippines.

TABLE 8

Annual Production of Selected Cereals in Countries Using New Seeds
(pounds per person of total population)

	India—Wheat	Pakistan—Wheat	Ceylon—Rice	Mexico— All Cereals
1960	53	87	201	495
1961	55	83	196	496
1962	59	87	213	525
1963	51	86	218	546
1964	46	83	213	611
1965	56	90	150	639
1966	46	71	188	649
1967	49	80	216	655
1968	76	116	247	680
1969	80	121	na	na

SOURCE: U.S. Dept. of Agriculture.

The case of Mexico can be examined more fully to provide some excellent clues to the relationship between rapid agricultural growth and improvement of income and diet. From 1900 to 1940, Mexico's agriculture was stagnant; daily caloric intake per person was estimated at 1,800 calories. Shortly thereafter, agriculture began to grow rapidly, averaging more than 5 per cent a year between 1940 and 1960; the economy grew at an annual rate of 6 per cent. As a result of this rapid and sustained growth in both food production and purchasing power, daily caloric intake in Mexico increased from 1,800 to 2,650 calories per person, an increase of nearly 50 per cent in 20 years. This does not mean that all Mexicans are well nourished today; as we saw in Chapter 9, a large segment of the population has been bypassed by the new technologies. But the average food-energy intake in the country is now well above the minimum established by nutritionists.

Taiwan is another place where agricultural progress has led to income growth and marked improvements in diet. In rural areas of West Pakistan wheat consumption is rising sharply as the new wheats spread; rice consumption is rising in the Philippine countryside as the new rices are planted there.

The relationship between malnutrition and poverty can also be demonstrated by considering how income changes affect patterns of food consumption. The preferred staple food of most of mankind is wheat or rice—wheat in the rich countries and a few poor countries, rice in most of the rest. Each of these grains supplies about one fifth of man's total food-energy supply. When wheat and rice are not available at a reasonable price, corn and sorghum take their place; when people cannot afford these coarse grains, they eat plantains, sweet potatoes, and cassava (tapioca). As Table 9 shows, the cheapest and least popular staples tend to be the least nutritious as well.

TABLE 9

Protein Content of Selected Food Staples

Food Staple	Protein Content (per cent)
Wheat (hard red spring)	14.0
Sorghum	11.0
Wheat (soft red winter)	10.2
Corn	8.9
Rice	7.5
Potatoes	2.1
Sweet potatoes	1.7
Bananas	1.1
Cassava	.6

As incomes rise, people consume more of their preferred staple food up to a point, whereupon dependence on a single starchy staple diminishes in favor of greater consumption of fruits and vegetables, vegetable oils, sugar, and, most important, livestock products. As incomes rise, more and more cereals are fed to livestock.

The average North American diet requires 1,700 pounds of grain annually, of which only 150 pounds are consumed directly in the form of bread, pastry, and breakfast cereals. The rest is consumed indirectly in the form of meat, milk, and eggs. In the poor countries, the average citizen has about 400 pounds of grain available to him each year. Allowing 10 per cent for seed, approximately one pound per day is available for consumption. Nearly all of this must be consumed directly to meet minimal food-energy requirements, leaving little for conversion into meat, milk, or eggs. As cereal supplies rise above this 400-pound threshold, more grain becomes available for conversion into protein.

FUTURE FOOD DEMANDS

In the poor countries a large percentage of income growth is used to buy food, whereas in rich countries only a minor share of increased income goes toward food purchases. Figure 4 illustrates on a global basis the relationship between grain use and income. As a rule of thumb, we can say that for every two-dollar increase in yearly income, grain use increases by one and a half pounds.

But future food-demand trends in the poor countries depend in part on how fast the new technologies raise incomes and in part on the course of food prices. During most of the 1960's food prices rose, as a result of three factors: lagging food production in the poor countries, a steady reduction in world grain reserves, and the decision by the United States government to dole out food aid more cautiously. As noted earlier, world rice prices climbed from $120 to $200 per ton

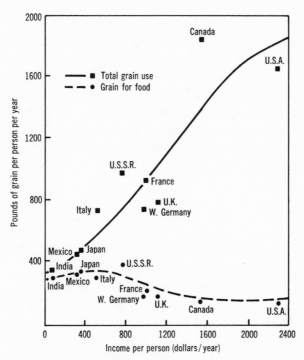

Source: U.S. Department of Agriculture. Data for 1959-61.

Figure 4. INCOME AND PER-CAPITA GRAIN CONSUMPTION

as a result of a worldwide shortage. Wheat prices also rose, affecting all of the large developing countries, India, Indonesia, Pakistan, and Brazil included. As was noted earlier, these higher prices were important in explaining the sudden adoption and rapid spread of the new seeds. But they also reduced food consumption, particularly among the lower-income groups, unable to offset the price rises by increasing food expenditures.

In 1968 and 1969, prices began to slacken. Easing of cereal prices should continue, permitting widespread advances in food consumption. The new seeds and prospective lower fertilizer prices should also reduce the cost of livestock products, particularly eggs and broilers, that are produced with grain.

In the case of Mexico, where the process of agricultural modernization began much earlier than in most other developing countries, crop prices declined an average of nearly 1 per cent a year from 1940 through 1962. The result was a substantial increase in the amount and variety of food consumed by the average Mexican over this one-generation span. The same thing could happen in more and more developing countries until hunger, as a prevailing condition, is largely eliminated. It could happen, that is, if incomes continue to rise rapidly enough and for a sufficient period of time, particularly if rising incomes are accompanied by declining cereal prices.

But rising incomes, while essential to the elimination of hunger and malnutrition in the poor countries in the long run, are not adequate to the immediate task. Protein hunger is much more costly to eliminate than caloric hunger. The conventional approach to raising the intake of high-quality protein—by expanding livestock production—is expensive and time-consuming. Techniques must be sought so that the world's poor can attain an adequate diet at a much earlier stage of development than has historically been the case. Fortunately, science is offering some attractive short cuts to dietary improvements. Only after considering these can we fashion a strategy to eliminate hunger in the 'seventies.

16

New Protein Sources

As we have noted, less than 10 per cent of the 1,700 pounds of grain the average American requires per year is consumed directly, whereas the average person in the poor countries has only 400 pounds of grain, nearly all of which must be consumed directly to keep body and soul together.

In the past, diets improved significantly only when grain supplies began to exceed direct consumption needs, leaving large quantities to be converted into high-protein livestock products. But this is a costly way of achieving high-quality diets. (See Figure 5.) If cereals could be reengineered or fortified so that their protein quality approached that of livestock protein, the cost of achieving high-quality diets could be greatly reduced.

Plant breeders, biochemists, food technologists, and microbiologists are responding to this challenge. With the new seeds and other materials to work with, they can hope to achieve an adequate diet with the resources available in the poor countries. New ideas just coming off the drawing boards will have a major impact on nutrition during the 1970's.

THE PROTEIN HUNTERS

Protein is made of amino acids, of which there are some twenty, including six that are essential to human nutrition. Individual plant proteins are low in quality because they

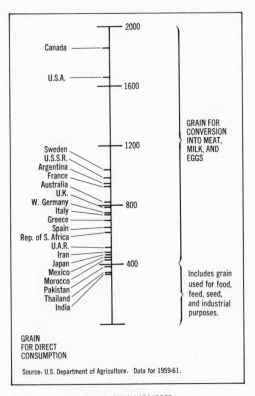

Figure 5. GRAIN USE LADDER
(Pounds of grain used per person per year)

lack one or more of the essential amino acids. Corn, for example, is deficient in lysine and, to a lesser extent, in tryptophane, both essential for human nutrition. Corn-consuming populations therefore suffer from a shortage of these amino acids in their diet. These deficiencies can be overcome either genetically or biochemically, through fortification of the corn itself.

The discovery of a high-lysine gene, Opaque 22, in a collection of corn germ plasm by Edwin T. Mertz and his associates at Purdue in 1963 opened a new front in man's efforts to combat malnutrition on a global scale. A description of this discovery in the July, 1964, issue of *Science* attracted the attention of scientists all over the world. Among them was Ulysses J. Grant, Director of the Rockefeller Agricultural Research Program in Colombia. Recognizing the implications of the Purdue discovery for Colombia, where corn is the staple food, and where protein malnutrition affects much of the population, Grant's chief corn breeder requested a seed sample from Purdue. From this sample, the Rockefeller scientists developed commercial corn varieties with a high-lysine content which were released for general use in 1969.

Tests in Colombia indicate that hogs fed with these high-protein corns gained weight twice as fast as those receiving only local corn. Similarly dramatic effects are being achieved with limited trials on human beings.

High-lysine corn has a great attraction in Latin America and in sub-Saharan Africa. The staple food in some 14 countries, corn accounts for at least half of the food-energy supply in Guatemala, Kenya, Rhodesia, Zambia, and Malawi. Diets will improve enormously if the new high-lysine corn varieties now being released commercially in Colombia, Kenya, and elsewhere replace traditional corn. Where the new corn is used as livestock feed, the need for costly protein supplements will be substantially reduced.

To realize the nutritional promise of high-lysine corn, plant breeders must incorporate it into commercial varieties without sacrificing too much yield potential. They must also eliminate some of its undesirable functional characteristics, such as a bitter taste, which reduces consumer acceptance. Progress to date suggests that none of these barriers is insuperable. The corn-protein breakthrough has created an awareness of the possibilities of improving cereal protein, triggering research efforts with other grains.

To the extent that high yield and high protein content can be incorporated in the same wheat and rice seeds, the prospect for expanding protein supplies are exciting indeed. Seeds that double yields and raise protein content by one fourth increase protein output per acre by 250 per cent!

The search for a high-yielding, high-protein rice variety analogous to the high-protein corn is under way at the International Rice Research Institute in the Philippines. With a vast collection of rice germ plasm already assembled, improving protein content is primarily a matter of testing, selecting, and breeding. When the right combination is found, it is bound to have a further dramatic impact on nutrition throughout Asia.

FORTIFYING PROTEINS

Scientists have invented ways of synthesizing amino acids economically, just as they had earlier synthesized vitamins. This in turn has made it possible to upgrade the quality of protein in cereals, for example, simply by adding the necessary amino acids. Adding four pounds of lysine to a ton of wheat costs only four dollars but results in one third more usable protein. Additions of essential amino acids to plant protein can make it equal in quality to animal protein.[1]

Government bakeries in the larger cities of India are now fortifying wheat flour with lysine, as well as with vitamins and minerals. Bread made with this flour may be the most nutritious marketed anywhere. It is quite literally the staff of life. Fully implemented, this program should result in the marketing of 100 million loaves of highly nutritious bread each year. Perhaps more important, it has stimulated private bakeries to fortify their bread as well.

Fortification with synthetic amino acids has a far-reaching commercial potential, both for food processing and for feed mixing. In the United States, lysine is now used in livestock feed, particularly for hogs, where it reduces the protein meal requirements and feed costs. As in the past, advanced nutri-

[1] Aaron Altschul, "Food Proteins for Humans," *Chemical and Engineering News,* November 24, 1969.

tional practices are being tried out on livestock and poultry before being used with humans. Japan is forging ahead in the use of lysine and other synthetic amino acids in both human food and livestock feed.

The USAID Mission in India is sponsoring, under the leadership of Alan Berg, studies of several novel ways to increase lysine intake. These include the possible use of salt and tea as carriers of lysine in much the same way salt is used as a carrier for iodine in the United States. Fortification of these two commodities, both widely consumed at all income levels, could prove a very effective way to upgrade the protein value of Indian diets.

A PROTEIN FOOD INDUSTRY

Paradoxically, in many poor countries, widespread protein hunger coexists with vast quantities of unused protein meals, largely the product of local vegetable-oil industries. In India, Nigeria, and other small countries, literally millions of tons of peanuts are produced for their oil, which is used in cooking. Other countries use coconut or soybean oil. After the seeds are crushed and the oil extracted, the meal remaining is largely protein. Unfortunately, little of this protein finds its way directly into the food stream, since most of the oil meal is fed to livestock or poultry, used for organic fertilizer, or exported to earn foreign exchange.

If some of the more than 20 million tons of peanut, cottonseed, coconut, and soybean meals available each year in the poor countries could be made into attractive, commercially successful protein foods, the result would be a major contribution toward the elimination of protein hunger. There are, however, some serious technical problems: the foods have to be made palatable, and toxic compounds have to be eliminated or prevented from forming. But these obstacles are slowly being overcome and some successful new products are beginning to appear.

Prominent among these are popular beverages being developed by several private firms using oilseed meals. Vitasoy, a soya-based beverage manufactured and marketed in Hong Kong, has captured one fourth of the soft-drink market there. A caramel-flavored beverage called Saci is now being introduced on a pilot basis by the Coca Cola Company in Brazil. Made of soybeans, caramel flavoring, sugar, and water—all indigenous to Brazil—this beverage is designed to have the nutritional value of milk. If it proves commercially viable in Brazil, the Coca Cola Company is expected to manufacture and market it in other poor countries. Puma, a banana-flavored protein drink designed by the Monsanto Corporation, is now manufactured and marketed in Guyana.

Eleven AID-financed investment surveys for high-protein food industries, using indigenous sources of protein, are under way in seven developing countries. Powdered protein mixes for beverages are being developed by Swift in Brazil and by Pillsbury in El Salvador. Other protein beverages and solid foods, nearly all using soya or cottonseed meal, are being designed and test-marketed elsewhere.

Experience in rich countries strongly suggests that the future of the protein food industry lies in developing substitutes for livestock products. Because of the high cost of livestock products, there are bound to be more and more substitutes appearing in the years ahead. So far, the substitutes have been developed and test-marketed in the rich countries, for the most part. The poor countries are only beginning to encourage investment in these industries, but as the demand for livestock products grows in these parts of the world, it is likely to be met more and more by substitutes.

The prime example of a successful livestock product substitute is oleomargarine. The hydrogenation process, by which vegetable oils are converted to solids at room temperature, permits large-scale substitution for animal fats, particularly butter and lard. Today the average American consumes eleven pounds of oleomargarine for every four pounds of butter, and lard is rarely found now in most American supermarkets. The primary reason for the substitution, of course, is much lower cost. This growing substitution for livestock products helps explain how the American farmer who was feeding 11 people in 1940, fed 35 in 1969.

Food technologists are now hard at work simulating such livestock products as milk and even meat. To the gourmet these may not sound very appetizing. The idea of getting meat from a mill that spins fibers from vegetable protein in the same way that synthetic textiles are spun is not calculated to make a French chef's mouth water. But by the time these fibers are colored, flavored, and pressed into forms that resemble ham or steak or chicken, they can fool most palates. And when the price drops below that charged for a pound of meat, housewives are likely to respond, perhaps accepting them as meat substitutes just as they accepted oleomargarine for butter.

One of the first commercial successes is a bacon substitute, now marketed throughout the United States. This product looks and tastes like bacon chips but is manufactured largely from soybeans, is high in protein and low in cholesterol, and requires neither cooking nor refrigeration. Pound for pound, it is quite competitive with cooked bacon. General Mills has broken ground for a plant in Cedar Rapids, Iowa, to be devoted solely to the production of this bacon substitute.

If bacon substitutes are followed by other pork substitutes, the lowly hog may become a curiosity to our grandchildren, to be seen only in zoos. The replacement of lard by vegetable shortenings has already radically altered the character of pork production, shifting the emphasis away from fat-type animals for lard to lean bacon-type hogs.

Imitation dairy products are gaining popularity throughout the United States. An estimated 65 per cent of all whipped toppings marketed in 1968 were of vegetable origin, coming from factories rather than dairy farms, as did 35 per cent of all coffee "creams" or whiteners. Imitation milks, either partly or wholly manufactured, are beginning to make inroads into fluid milk markets, particularly in the Southwest. The cow is slowly being supplanted by new processes of converting materials of plant origin directly into substitute dairy products. The net effect, of course, is a steady reduction in the agricultural resources needed to provide a given level of nutrition.

There is an interesting parallel between the position of high-protein foods in the poor countries today and that of low-calorie foods in the United States a decade ago. During the late 'fifties, when many overweight Americans were seeking easy ways to reduce caloric intake, a new technology evolved in response to this need as it was expressed in the marketplace, creating the low-calorie food industry. Today a wide range of low-calorie foods is available to American consumers, and a new industry has developed. Similarly, the need for more protein in the poor countries may well create a major new industry as new food technologies evolve.

The production of imitation livestock products is already spreading rapidly from the United States to Europe and Japan, where meat prices are high and low-cost substitutes are especially appealing. Some consumers in the poor countries could move directly from a grain diet to a meat-substitute diet if these products were available. In fact, the prospects for the protein food industry in the poor countries are particularly good, for the simple reason that there is little hope that incomes will rise fast enough or soon enough to permit extensive development of a livestock agriculture like that in the United States, except for purposes of export.

American cattlemen have adopted a novel compromise between traditional and unconventional technologies in the production of beef, the most popular source of animal protein in American diets. They are feeding urea, commonly used as a nitrogen fertilizer, to cattle as a means of reducing the need for protein concentrates and thus lowering the costs of beef production. In 1968, some 300,000 tons of urea were fed to cattle in the United States, more than is used as fertilizer in many countries. By feeding urea, farmers can reduce the protein content of other rations and rely heavily on low-cost roughage, such as cornstalks, corncobs, straw, and even sawdust. To make them palatable, the roughages are combined with molasses. Microorganisms in the rumen combine the nitrogen and carbohydrates to form protein, which the cattle can then absorb.

Where there is an adequate supply of roughage in the United States, as in the corn belt, feeding urea to cattle significantly reduces the cost of beef production. But this method should result in even greater economies in the tropics, where low-cost roughage can be produced easily all year round.

Far-out Foods

The threat of famine and widespread food shortage in the 1960's sparked investigation into two potential new sources of protein. One was the ocean; the other, the petroleum industry.

The idea of using algae as food was presented by science-fiction author Jules Verne more than a century ago. It is technically feasible to do so, but little progress has been achieved toward making algae a tasty commercial food product. Another food from the sea, with better prospects of success, is fish-protein concentrate. It can be processed from species of fish that are not usually consumed by humans, and that therefore are relatively inexpensive. Neutral in taste and color, it can be added directly to other dishes to boost protein intake, avoiding the difficulty of changing eating habits. But soy protein concentrate can do these things, too, at much lower cost with current technologies.

Perhaps the most exotic approach to expanding world protein supplies is the experimental effort to use petroleum as a feedstock for some of the simplest forms of plant life, such as yeast and other single-cell organisms. Now that its technical feasibility has been established, this idea is being intensively researched by more than a score of multinational petroleum companies. British Petroleum is constructing a small plant in France, which is expected to produce 16,000 tons of protein a year when completed, in 1970. The Soviet Union, chronically short of feedstuffs, is reportedly producing single-cell protein (SCP) of feed quality on a limited scale. Japan is now moving rapidly toward large-scale commercial production, expecting to produce more than 300,000 tons yearly by the end of 1971.

Promoters of SCP hope that it will eventually be suitable for humans, but the process currently in use appears to produce protein suitable only for livestock. Should this technology ever become firmly established, it would have far-reaching implications for conventional agriculture. And how ironic it is; photosynthesis, occurring eons ago, produced plant material that was eventually converted into petroleum; new technology has made it possible for that solar energy to be unlocked to compete directly with photosynthesis occurring on our farms today.

VI

Preview of the 1970's

17

The Self-Sufficiency Syndrome

The new seeds are making self-sufficiency in the local cereal a national status symbol, like the international airline or the steel mill a decade ago. Politicians in poor countries don't like to be dependent on food handouts from abroad; to many of them, self-sufficiency is now equated with political independence.

After years of steadily growing reliance on food aid from abroad, many poor countries that are using the new seeds are suddenly finding themselves approaching self-sufficiency in their basic cereal. Poor countries with a combined population of one billion people are expecting to attain self-sufficiency in their staple food by 1973 (Table 10).

With the introduction of the new seeds, countries that were chronic underachievers in agriculture are becoming overachievers, often before they are ready for the problems that self-sufficiency brings. Pakistan, for example, was aiming at self-sufficiency in cereals by 1972 but now expects to reach it in 1970. In India, continuation of the cereal-production trend of the past few years should bring self-sufficiency by 1972. Indonesia, now rapidly expanding production of both corn and rice, is planning to export corn in 1970 and to eliminate the need for rice imports within three years.

Smaller countries such as Ceylon and Malaysia used to import up to half of their rice requirements, paying for it from the proceeds of tea and rubber exports. But now these

TABLE 10
Attaining Self-Sufficiency in Cereal Staples

Self-Sufficiency Status	Crop	Year
Achieved		
Mexico	Wheat	1957
Kenya	Corn	1966
Iran	Wheat	1967
Philippines	Rice	1968
Pakistan	Rice	1968
Planned		
Afghanistan	Wheat	1970
Turkey	Wheat	1970
Pakistan	Wheat	1970
India	Wheat	1972
India	Rice	1972
Malaysia	Rice	1973
Ceylon	Rice	1973
Indonesia	Rice	1973

countries, too, are jumping on the self-sufficiency bandwagon. The increasing popularity of synthetic substitutes and the growing number of competitors in the markets for traditional tropical commodities are forcing these countries to seek self-sufficiency in their staple food.

Insofar as the politics of self-sufficiency increases the momentum of the Green Revolution, this is good. However, the drive for self-sufficiency raises a whole new set of problems. First, the production drive required to achieve self-sufficiency usually overshoots the target and results in large surpluses. Secondly, when countries new to the world market try to export these surpluses, they often find that they are not competitive in price, that they cannot meet the export subsidies of their competitors, or that they are trying to export a quality of cereal not in demand on the world market (e.g., they may offer soft wheats when the market wants hard wheats). Then, as storage facilities overflow and prices drop, there is a frantic effort to diversify, to shift land to crops other than cereals. But diversification requires new sets of inputs and different marketing systems, requirements that cannot be met quickly. At this point some countries turn to poultry and livestock production, feeding surplus grains to chickens, cattle, and pigs. This is a logical and necessary evolution, but it takes time, advance planning, new techniques, and many adjustments.

This characteristic sequence of frustrations is termed the self-sufficiency syndrome. More than one country has miscalculated the consequences of reaching self-sufficiency. In view of the likelihood that surpluses will begin to appear in many poor countries in the years immediately ahead, an understanding of the problem is essential. Some understanding can be fashioned out of the mistakes others have made. The new seeds do make farm diversification a somewhat easier task, but unless the rich countries open up their markets to more farm exports from the poor countries, self-sufficiency may turn out to be a hollow victory.

EXPORTABLE SURPLUSES

Some poor countries are already establishing export markets for their new surpluses. Perhaps the most successful in penetrating overseas markets is Thailand, which has developed a large and growing market for corn in Japan. It now ranks among the top five corn exporters in the world.

Mexico has recently exported small quantities of wheat, corn, and rice. Iran exported wheat in 1967 and 1968, its first successful penetration of the world wheat market. Since the new high-yielding wheat varieties were not introduced in Iran until early 1969, the prospects are good that Iran will be able to build on this new market in the future. The dramatic wheat-production gains in Pakistan may shortly bring that country into the wheat export market as well.

The Philippines exported a modest tonnage of rice in 1968, mostly to Indonesia. But the future of Philippine rice exports is uncertain. Not only has IR-8 rice a limited appeal to importers, but unless Japan lowers its own exorbitant price support for rice and again becomes a major importer, Southeast Asia has little hope of developing much export business in rice.

Brazil, a marginal exporter of both rice and corn in recent years, increased its exports of corn to a million tons in 1968, double the previous record. In view of its vast underutilized farm resources, Brazil could become a leading feed-grain exporter in the years ahead, especially if it continues to import most of its wheat. However, again the prospect depends on a reordering of the world cereal markets to permit new entrants. Ironically, to achieve and maintain an exportable surplus of cereals means for most poor countries another kind of dependence on the rich: there must be export markets. This is a much healthier kind of dependence than continued reliance on food aid, but it is nonetheless dependence. No nation is entirely independent in today's world, not even the United States. What the poor countries need and probably will demand ever more insistently in the 'seventies is the right to earn more of their way in the world through access to export markets where they have a comparative advantage. We shall return to this subject in Chapter 20, with some suggestions about how this access might be worked out.

Farm Diversification

When attempts to export cereal surpluses are frustrated, either because the products are not competitive or because the rich countries insist on maintaining economic barriers to imports, the poor countries turn to diversification—and often to more frustrations.

We have noted that the new seeds, with their early maturity and reduced sensitivity to day length, facilitate diversification because they create new possibilities for multiple cropping. Short-season crops can be sown between the rice and wheat crops when there is an adequate supply of controlled water. Diversification can be aimed either at the home market or the export market.

As incomes rise in the poor countries, there will be steadily growing markets for vegetables and fruits, many of which can be included in a multicropping regimen. But the real gains in the short run are more likely to come in the export market, again provided that the rich countries cooperate. The range of fruits and vegetables that can be produced in the tropical-subtropical regions is generally much greater than that of the temperate zones.

As incomes rise in industrial countries, lucrative markets open up for imported fruits and vegetables. These markets are already important sources of foreign exchange for Turkey, Israel, Mexico, Taiwan, the Philippines, and Chile. Japan's removal of restrictions on banana imports in 1963 created new banana export industries in nearby countries in East Asia. Taiwan's exports of bananas, a few million dollars a year in 1955, soared to $55 million in 1965, following Japanese import liberalization. The Philippines and Malaysia are also taking advantage of the growing Japanese market.

As modern transport, such as the jumbo jets, are more widely used, the possibilities for exporting fresh fruits and vegetables will expand. High-value products, such as strawberries and lettuce, are now being flown several thousand miles from producer to market. New highways are also linking areas of potential production with world markets, the classic example being the Friendship Highway in Thailand referred to earlier. The newly paved road that passes through Afghanistan and the Khyber Pass and links Pakistan with the Soviet Union and the Middle East is opening an entirely new market for Pakistani farmers. The Soviet Union could become an important outlet for Pakistan's winter fruits and vegetables, much as the United States is for Mexico. The tropical-subtropical countries, with their year-round growing conditions, can complement the production patterns of the industrial countries in the temperate zone, especially during the winter season.

Many poor countries, lacking the marketing and processing know-how to gain access to overseas markets, are attracting investments by multinational food-processing corporations that have the global marketing systems needed to link the production resources of these countries with foreign markets. The Philippines pineapple industry is a good example. Investments in pineapple processing by two large American firms, Dole and Del Monte, have enabled the Philippines to capture a share of the world processed-pineapple market.

Taiwan and Mexico, two developing countries with outstanding agricultural growth records, are diversifying rapidly. The situations in these countries illustrate the close relationship between rapid agricultural growth and diversification. In 1950 sugar accounted for 80 per cent of Taiwan's total exports and almost all of its agricultural exports. By 1967, sugar exports, though still large, accounted for only 7 per cent of a greatly expanded total; banana exports, largely to Japan, accounted for 10 per cent. Exports of canned fruits and vegetables, quite modest in the 1950's, had climbed to $84 million in 1967, including principally canned mushrooms, asparagus, and pineapple. The diversification of Taiwan's agriculture is a dynamic, continuing process, with new crops continually being introduced for export.

Mexico's agriculture diversified rapidly during the 'sixties. After self-sufficiency in wheat was reached, the Mexican government discovered that internal prices were well above world market prices. It then began shifting its resources into the production of corn, sorghum, and soybeans, thereby expanding the grain-based poultry and livestock industries. Corn production increased from 6.4 million tons in 1963 to nine million tons in 1968; production of sorghum and soybeans multiplied several fold. The production of processed fruits and vegetables, intended primarily for export to the United States during the off season, also expanded rapidly in this period. Production of strawberries, reaching 140 million pounds in 1968, nearly tripled, as did production of watermelons and cantaloupes.

Mexico and Taiwan are good examples of countries which overcame the frustrations of the self-sufficiency syndrome. Pakistan could be the next; in addition to good export prospects for fruits and vegetables, Pakistan is developing a promising peanut agriculture, doubling production between 1966 and 1968. The growth of peanut cultivation means a reduced need to import vegetable oils and the prospect of using peanut oilmeal in the livestock feed industry. Kenya and Brazil are two other countries where diversification is proceeding at an encouraging pace.

POULTRY AND LIVESTOCK

The final stage of the self-sufficiency syndrome is the expansion of poultry and livestock production. As countries using the new seeds reach self-sufficiency in food grains, feed grains acquire new status. The expanding availability of low-cost grains, plus the continuing spread of modern poultry and livestock production techniques, make a poultry-livestock boom almost certain. How quickly this prospect materializes depends on whether governments can effectively combine economic policies and new technologies, as they did to get cereal production moving.

At present, consumption of poultry and livestock meat in poor countries often amounts to only a few pounds per person yearly. This is a minute fraction of the 120 pounds of meat (excluding poultry) consumed yearly in the European Economic Community and the 180 pounds in the United States. In the poultry-livestock sector, production of broilers is likely to expand most rapidly. Modern broiler-production technologies developed in the United States since World

War II are adaptable throughout the world, with only minimal modification for local conditions. With little investment in research, poor countries can take advantage of the cumulative American investment in poultry nutrition, breeding, pathology, and flock management.

For the poor countries, poultry husbandry has several advantages over livestock. With modern production techniques, grain-fed poultry costs less than grain-fed pork or beef, since feed requirements per pound of meat are much lower. A well-managed broiler flock requires only three pounds of grain per pound. The rule of thumb for converting grain into meat indicates four pounds of grain are required to produce one pound of pork and seven for a pound of beef.

The dramatic gains in efficiency in broiler production achieved since World War II far exceed the gains with cattle or hogs. In poor countries, where feed resources are relatively scarce, and in countries, such as Japan, that depend on imported feed materials, policies are increasingly being designed to encourage the development of a poultry industry, sometimes at the expense of beef and dairy.

Another attraction of poultry is the short payout period. Chicks hatch in only 21 days. With modern management and feed, broilers are ready to market within ten to twelve weeks, enabling investors to recoup their capital quickly. Chickens also have a distinct marketing advantage since they are small and can be consumed almost immediately after slaughter.

How rapidly poultry production expands depends in part on how rapidly the feed-mixing industry expands. American feed companies have often taken the lead in introducing modern broiler and egg production, since this helps to expand the market for commercially mixed feeds. The establishment of hatcheries to produce high-quality chicks will also encourage the formation of a broiler industry. Leading hatcheries have already established their breeding lines in many poor countries.

Over time, as the number of consumers who can afford poultry multiplies, modern broiler production spreads from the outskirts of larger cities to smaller ones, and subsequently to towns and villages. In addition to the growth in poultry consumption due to rising incomes, modern broiler-production techniques often reduce the price from something like 80 cents per pound to about 50 cents, bringing it within the reach of a far larger group of consumers.

Rapid expansion of production is not readily achieved with livestock or pork. This is not only because the life cycle of these animals is longer, but also because pasture improvement, the construction of small dams for water retention and flood control, and the acquisition of better breeding stock are time-consuming projects. Nevertheless, the general trend is illustrated by a recent report from the United States agricultural attaché in the Philippines: "With self-sufficiency in rice and corn achieved, at least temporarily, resources are being diverted to secondary crops [and] livestock. . . ."

Sharp increases in corn production in Andra Pradesh, an agricultural state in eastern India, are encouraging the formation of a commercial hog industry. In Mexico and Kenya, both now exporting grain, the shift toward livestock is well under way.

Rising incomes at home and expanding export prospects abroad are major stimuli for the expansion of livestock herds. Efforts to convert the grazing potential of Latin America and sub-Saharan Africa into exports are being assisted by substantial loans from the World Bank, AID, and the Inter-American Development Bank. At the end of 1966, livestock improvement ranked third, after irrigation and farm credit, as a World Bank loan activity in agriculture. Another indication of the planned expansion and upgrading of cattle production in poor countries is the sharp increase in exports of American breeding cattle, from $12 million in 1960 to $24 million in 1967, most of it going to Latin America.

IMPLICATIONS OF SELF-SUFFICIENCY

Achievement of cereal self-sufficiency is not without cost. It requires more foreign exchange to finance needed inputs of fertilizer and other agricultural prerequisites to maintain than does dependence on food aid. And as we have seen, this is not the only frustration associated with becoming self-sufficient.

How far and how fast the Green Revolution progresses will depend heavily on whether rich countries are prepared to modify their protectionist policies to allow more grain imports from poor countries. At present, the rich countries do not seem eager to welcome them into the world grain markets.

18

The New Seeds and the American Farmer

The new seeds are having an impact that extends far beyond the borders of the countries where they are being planted. Designed specifically to capitalize on the greater supply of solar energy and the year-round growing temperatures of the tropics, they are strengthening the comparative advantage of the tropical-subtropical countries in cereal production. Poor countries, until recently grain importers, are appearing with increasing frequency on the export side of the ledger.

Even without knowing exactly how the new technologies will reorder world agricultural trade, we can already see the beginnings of significant change. The recent production gains in the poor countries challenge all the rich countries, particularly the more protectionist ones in Europe, and Japan, as we shall discuss in Chapter 19. They challenge the American farmer in a very different way. He must adjust to declining levels of food-aid exports, principally wheat, while simultaneously adjusting to expanding opportunities for commercial exports of the wide range of commodities he produces so efficiently.

THE CHANGING TRADE PATTERN

The implications of the Green Revolution for the American farmer are best understood in their historical context. During the three decades ending in 1966, world cereal trade was characterized by the growing dependence of the poor countries on cereal imports and North America's emergence as the world's breadbasket. North America exported five million tons a year 30 years ago but nearly 60 million tons in 1966 (Table 11).

TABLE 11

The Changing Pattern of World Grain Trade
(million metric tons)

Region	1934–38	1948–52	1960	1966
North America	+ 5	+23	+39	+59
Latin America	+ 9	+ 1	0	+ 5
Western Europe	−24	−22	−25	−27
Eastern Europe & U.S.S.R.	+ 5	*	0	− 4
Africa	+ 1	0	− 2	− 7
Asia	+ 2	− 6	−17	−34
Australia & New Zealand	+ 3	+ 3	+ 6	+ 8

* Not available
SOURCE: U.S. Department of Agriculture.

Converging, sometimes unrelated global trends contributed to North America's increasing dominance of the world grain market. Beginning in World War II, science was applied to agriculture in the United States and Canada on a broad scale. It was successful enough to enable these two countries to export almost 60 million tons of grain a year while the United States was withholding 50 million acres of crop land from production to avoid glutting world markets! In Asia, Africa, and Latin America, meanwhile, the need for food, spurred by rapid population growth, far outstripped agricultural growth, turning food surpluses into food deficits. In Eastern Europe and the Soviet Union, historically exporters of grain, emerging food deficits were due more to the mismanagement of agriculture.

Mainland China, afflicted by both population growth and the ill effects of Mao's communalization of Chinese agriculture, became a major food importer in 1961. Since then it has consistently imported four to six million tons of grain yearly.

A unique combination of technological, political, demographic, and economic forces converged to give North America a near-monopoly of world grain exports by 1966. The current degree of dominance is not likely to continue indefinitely. This is not to say that North America's cereal exports will decline, only that its share of the total will not always be as large as it has been in some recent years.

Available data provide only fragmentary and very unreliable indications of the future changes in the pattern of agricultural trade that will come as a result of the spread of the new seeds. Perhaps the most interesting statistic suggests a major shift in the destination of American farm exports. In 1968 Asia replaced Europe as the leading export market for the United States. This was due in part to rising protectionism in Europe, and in part to economic growth in several Asian countries.

Shifts in rice trade reflect in microcosm some of the broader shifts in global agricultural trade. Throughout the modern era the Southeast Asian "rice bowl"—Burma, Thailand, and, to a lesser extent, Cambodia and Vietnam—has supplied most of the rice entering the world market. During the 1960's, Southeast Asia lost its pre-eminence in this area. The war in Vietnam and, until recently, lagging rice production in the food-aid recipient countries encouraged American rice producers to expand their acreage in the mid-sixties. This enabled the United States to edge Thailand out as the world's leading rice exporter in 1968.

Meanwhile, the Indus Plain of West Pakistan, with the new rices, its controlled water supply, and its abundance of solar energy, may become the rice bowl of the future, challenging both Southeast Asia and the United States. How successful Pakistan will be in parlaying its agronomic advantage into a commanding position in the world market remains to be seen. To do so, it must be able, not only to undersell its competition, but also to satisfy the quality demands of various importing countries. In any case, Pakistan, which has recently become a net rice exporter, is likely to provide keen competition in a world market that faces a rapidly shrinking volume of buyers and, when peace comes to Vietnam, a rejuvenated list of traditional sellers.

The new rices and the possibilities for multiple cropping they offer in rotation with feed grains are likely to generate exportable surpluses of feed grains in a number of tropical-subtropical countries within the next few years. Among countries likely to be competing for the projected growth in the world feed-grain market are Brazil, Mexico, Kenya, Thailand, Indonesia, and the Philippines.

DECLINING FOOD AID

During the mid-sixties, two fifths of the American wheat crop was shipped abroad as food aid, one fifth to India alone. Another fifth was exported commercially. Food-aid shipments in 1964 exceeded 500 million bushels, but by 1968 they had declined 45 per cent (Table 12).

TABLE 12

Wheat Exports Under the U.S. Food Aid Program

Year	Bushels (millions)	Year	Bushels (millions)
1954	15	1962	370
1955	132	1963	461
1956	253	1964	509
1957	243	1965	449
1958	219	1966	461
1959	254	1967	342
1960	381	1968	283
1961	384		

SOURCE: U.S. Department of Agriculture.

If Pakistan should become self-sufficient in cereal production in 1970, as scheduled, and if India should follow within a year or two, then food aid could drop much lower, requiring continuing structural adjustments in American agriculture.

Continuation of food aid is not justified if it artificially depresses grain prices in poor countries that are just now experiencing a production breakthrough. Carroll G. Brunthaver, a senior USDA official, recently suggested that legislation governing food aid might soon be changed:

> PL 480 is now 15 years old. . . . It is scheduled to expire at the end of [1970]. . . . As we move forward under PL 480 it is important to remember that aid programs can and should be used to expand commercial trade. They should not be used to perpetuate a relationship of dependency between countries. I am not being coldhearted. I am simply taking the view that there is no profit for anyone in a policy of permanent charity. There is no future in being a permanent benefactor. And there is no future for the dependent country in such a relationship.[1]

Mr. Brunthaver could have added that with the advent of the new seeds, there is less and less justification for continued dependence by the poor countries on massive food aid.

What is needed, basically, is an international agreement among the developed countries to share the burdens of overproduction in grains in ways that permit expanding world trade and expanding production in the poor countries. A specific recommendation on this subject is presented in Chapter 20.

As a means of balancing the supply and demand of grain, food aid is more costly to the Treasury than simply paying farmers to take land out of production. The net income to the farmer may be the same whether he produces wheat or is paid not to produce it, since the payment for nonproduction usually approximates his net income. A bushel of wheat shipped abroad as food aid costs the Treasury nearly two

[1] Carroll Brunthaver, speech before American Corn Millers' Association, Washington, D. C., October 16, 1959.

dollars, including shipping charges borne by the United States; paying the farmer not to produce a bushel of wheat costs less than a dollar.

Declines in food aid, coming at the same time that the trend of rising farm exports to Europe has been arrested by protectionism, are resulting in reduced acreages of food grains in the United States. Wheat-acreage allotments, expanded in 1967 to cope with scarcity, were reduced 13 per cent in 1968, and 12 per cent in 1969, and 12 per cent in 1970. Rice acreage, reduced 10 per cent in 1969, will probably be reduced further in 1970. These acreage reductions do not result in a loss in farm income if diversion payments are high enough.

What *is* lost is a great deal of farm-related business, especially in the Northern Great Plains, where much of the wheat is grown and where local economies depend on business generated by the production, marketing, and storage of wheat. Farm-supply and service industries in rural communities suffer when wheat acreage is reduced. The rural communities derive some benefit from diversion payments made to farmers who take acreage out of production. They may not suffer any loss if farmers shift from wheat to feed grains or to beef cattle, for which there has been a buoyant demand for many years. Nonetheless, when the government shifts gears in agricultural policy, especially when it shifts to a lower gear, the effect in the rural areas is inevitably unsettling.

U.S. FARM EXPORT PROSPECTS

In all probability, some sort of food-aid program will be continued for many years, if only to ensure a quick response in the event of international emergencies or disasters requiring massive relief efforts. But food aid for emergencies will be much less than the food-aid programs undertaken in the 'sixties. The slack must be taken up by increased commercial exports.

At first glance, it might appear that the trend toward self-sufficiency in wheat or rice in the poor countries would throttle growth in world trade in farm products and damage United States export prospects in particular. But this is not necessarily so. In many temperate-zone farm products, the American producer is the most efficient in the world. As incomes rise, consumers everywhere demand a much greater variety of food. For example, the United States, despite its highly productive farm sector and varied climate and crops, imports four billion dollars' worth of farm products yearly. The average supermarket displays 7,000 different food items on its shelves. As incomes rise in the poor countries, consumers there will demand an ever-wider variety of food products, many of which the United States can supply.

The increasing diversity of diets is reflected even in such basics as cereal consumption. Although the Philippines has achieved self-sufficiency in rice, for example, it is importing steadily growing tonnages of wheat. Indonesia may achieve self-sufficiency in rice and become an exporter of feed grains, but, like the Philippines, it must import more and more wheat to satisfy consumer demand as incomes resume their rise. Densely populated Taiwan, long an exporter of rice, imports growing quantities of wheat and even more rapidly growing quantities of feed grains, the latter to meet its soaring demand for the poultry and pork that higher incomes demand.

The modernization of agriculture in the poor countries will, of course, provide new competition for American farm products in some instances. But modernization is also the key to export expansion. It is precisely those countries that have recorded outstanding performances in agriculture during the 1960's that have rapidly increased their imports from the United States. Table 13 shows that farm imports over the past decade virtually tripled in all countries with outstanding performances in agriculture, with the exception of Mexico.

Japan's farm imports have tripled despite its achievement of self-sufficiency in rice during this period.

TABLE 13

Commercial Agricultural Exports of the United States to Countries with Outstanding Agricultural Performances
(millions of dollars)

Country	1956–60 Average	1966	1967
Japan	335	900	863
South Korea	10	20	42
Taiwan	4	30	68
Pakistan	5	9	13
Israel	10	44	38
Mexico	69	79	70
Total	433	1082	1094

Studies show a close relationship between income levels abroad and imports of farm products from the United States. Countries with per-capita incomes of more than $600 a year bought $7.80 worth of farm products per person in 1964. Where average income was between $200 and $600, sales averaged $4.18 per person. Where incomes were under $200 a year, sales were a mere 30 cents per person. In Japan, for example, where national income expanded nearly 9 per cent a year between 1962 and 1967, purchases of United States farm products increased from $480 million to $863 million.

The American farmer should welcome the Green Revolution. Adjusting to the impact of the new seeds and the associated technologies will require forward planning; it will require practicing the ancient art of diplomacy with more skill than ever before, and it will require a reorientation of market-development efforts abroad to capitalize on the new opportunities created by the new seeds. Perhaps most important, it will require a generous and efficient foreign-aid program just at the time when the public seems most disenchanted with the idea.

Again we return to the central challenge of the Green Revolution: the new seeds make the prospect of rising incomes and purchasing power in the poor countries much more realistic than ever before. But it is still only a prospect. Given the fact that the whole world will benefit if it is realized, it is only common sense to urge that the United States do what it can to make this possibility a reality.

From the point of view of the American farmer, this is a matter of simple self-interest. Strengthening the economic position of the poor countries means in effect substituting commercial for concessional exports, putting exports on a much firmer basis, more dependent on the American farmer's ability to compete and less dependent on the political vagaries of government. Asia's new position as the leading regional market for America's farm produce is but one indication of the growing importance of the less-developed world for the American farmer. Significantly, Asia's displacement of Europe occurred despite the Green Revolution and the sharp decline in food-aid shipments to the region!

19

Rising Agricultural Protectionism

Agriculture should lend itself more to international trade than many other economic activities do simply because each country has a unique combination of soils, climate, and rainfall. As incomes rise, trade should expand. But the record of the 1960's has been one of increasing protectionism and increasingly distorted production patterns. The share of the world's food supply contributed by high-cost, inefficient producers has increased rapidly, and often at the expense of the more efficient producers. If this trend persists in the 'seventies, it could embitter relations among countries in some disturbing ways.

Europe, insisting on growing more and more of its own food regardless of the cost to its consumers or to producers elsewhere, has accumulated burdensome surpluses of cereals and dairy products and is approaching a crisis unless it adjusts its agricultural policies. The case for agricultural protectionism is made concisely in the basic handbook on agricultural policy distributed by the European Economic Community.

The Community's basic premise is that every country uses its agricultural policy as a means of support for its farmers, though with varying methods. Support may take the form of subsidies, import duties or levies, quantitative restrictions . . . and so on. All these forms of support are reflected in the price the producer receives for his product.

This is, indeed, conventional wisdom, of a sort that the United States began to discard a decade ago, when it found that high support prices for commodities could all too easily lead to large surpluses, costly to produce and to export. We found that the system would not work without production controls, but Europe and Japan have not yet faced this fact. They are only now learning that the social cost of subsidies for farm products can burden taxpayers and consumers heavily without helping the farmer in any substantial way.

The direct budgetary costs of the EEC's Common Agricultural Policy in 1969, for example, approached eight billion dollars. If the premium over world market prices that European consumers pay for their staple foods is added to that figure, the total cost to taxpayers and consumers exceeds $14 billion.[1] Nor is this huge social cost appreciably improving the the lot of the European farmer.

In 1969 West Germany, for example, was imposing an import duty of 76 per cent on wheat. Its duties on imported feed grains ranged from 73 per cent for corn to 83 per cent for barley. It is not surprising that European cereal prices are nearly double world levels, or that the German livestock producer pays almost exactly twice as much for feed grains as his American counterpart.

Expensive as feed grains are under the Common Market's agricultural policy, European dairy farmers still find it profitable to convert them into butter. With the support price for butter at nearly one dollar a pound, these farmers have produced a surplus of 660 million pounds! A West German legislator, who had the thankless task of defending the appropria-

---

[1] George R. Kruer and Byron Bernston, "Cost of the Common Agricultural Policy to the European Community," *Foreign Agricultural Trade of the United States,* U.S. Department of Agriculture, October, 1969, pp. 6–12.

tions bill for the butter subsidy in his country, described its essential irrationality in very down-to-earth terms:

> First you take the milk from the calf which the calf would normally get and make butter out of it; then you turn around and put the butter in a milk replacer and give it back to the calf, having spent an awful lot of money in the meantime.

In 1969 the direct budgetary costs of supporting dairy products alone in the EEC will approach $800 million. A good portion of this will go to subsidize exports, for the EEC is now dumping butter on the world market at 20 cents a pound, absorbing 80 per cent of the domestic cost with an export subsidy. The consumer-taxpayer, of course, pays coming and going.

Rising agricultural protectionism in Europe and Japan is in part the result of catering to large rural representations in politics: within the EEC it is in a real sense part of the cement holding the Six together. It will not be easy in Japan or in the Common Market for political leaders to back away from past policies. However, it must be a primary objective of American agricultural diplomacy to help them do just that.

Cost to the Poor Countries

It can be argued, although not very persuasively, that one of the luxuries the rich can afford is inefficiency, even on the scale represented by current agricultural policies in Europe and Japan. The poor countries can support no such luxury. They must have a rational system of trade in farm products through which they can hope to earn more of their way in the world.

But when surpluses from the rich countries are dumped on the world market at a price well below the cost of production, the poor countries lose this opportunity. The pending crisis in the world rice market is a case in point.

The exceedingly high world price of rice, which reached

$200 a ton in 1967 and early 1968, triggered a global production response. Only a small share of the world rice crop—less than 3 per cent of the harvest—enters the world market. This means that even modest variations in exportable surpluses cause wide swings in price. With the rapid spread of high-yielding rices moving more countries into the world market as exporters, it becomes easy to forecast future price trends: the world price is almost certainly going to continue the decline under way in 1969.

Here is where agricultural protectionism in the rich countries really hurts. Japan and Russia, for example, were substantial rice importers as recently as the mid-1960's. In 1969 Japan actually exported some rice, and the Soviet Union, which recently has been importing 200,000–400,000 tons a year, plans to be self-sufficient by 1970. What, then, is the prospect for Pakistan and the Philippines, both of which are turning rice deficits into exportable surpluses, thanks to the Green Revolution?

Rice is the most dramatic example, but other cereals are affected in the same fashion. France's exportable surplus of four and a half million tons of barley had to be marketed outside the Common Market with an enormous subsidy as did its exports of wheat. If Pakistan's effort to export soft wheats in the early 'seventies materializes and becomes a matter of competing subsidies between the French and Pakistani treasuries, there can be little doubt of the outcome despite Pakistan's comparative advantage.

REPEALING THE CORN LAWS

There is no more immediate and urgent test of the rich countries' intentions toward the poor countries in the decade ahead than how they tackle the thorny problem of agricultural protectionism. The choices are not easy ones. The rich, for example, could increase their direct financial aid to the poor as a substitute for permitting more exports of farm prod-

ucts. But this is hardly likely to be a popular solution among
the taxpayers of the rich countries. Why should they pay
higher food prices, be taxed to pay direct subsidies to their
own farmers, and, finally, provide "foreign aid" to offset the
adverse effects of agricultural protectionism on the poor
countries? The case for more aid is very strong, as we will
show in Chapter 20, but the argument of using it to offset
protectionism is less than persuasive.

We might hope that there will be more "consumer reac-
tion" within the rich countries against highly protectionist
farm policies. The editorial writers of the *Manchester Guardian* recently challenged their neighbors in Europe by asking
"whether a system designed primarily to protect farmers
instead of consumers is appropriate to an industrial continent
in the twentieth century." The *Guardian* argued that the
basic premise underlying agricultural policy should be not
"to support farmers" but "to provide food at the most economic cost." The distinguished newspaper was harking back
to a famous debate that took place in Britain a century and
a quarter ago and led to the repeal of Britain's highly protec-
tive Corn Laws.

The kinds of considerations that might creep into such a
debate were illustrated recently when a group of Dutch stu-
dents, in response to the global poverty problem, organized
a boycott of beet sugar in their country. If economics alone
prevailed, there would be little if any beet sugar produced
in the world; sugar would come from cane, virtually all of it
from the tropical and subtropical countries. Beet sugar costs
between seven and ten cents a pound to produce, while cane
sugar costs only two to four cents. The United States took
a big step backward toward protectionism in the 1960's by
sharply reducing its imports of sugar in favor of more costly
domestic production, much of it from beets.

In fact, if there is to be a great debate against the modern
Corn Laws in the 1970's, the United States will be in a some-

what stronger position than European countries, Japan, or even Great Britain. It has assumed almost single-handedly the responsibility for stabilizing the prices of wheat and feed grains in the world markets by withholding a vast acreage of crop land from production. Since governments are much too deeply involved in agriculture to permit any approach to genuine free trade, the outcome of debate against the Corn Laws today will depend on the willingness of the European and Japanese governments to divert resources from production, through either direct controls or indirect ones, by lowering domestic support prices. Our ability to effect such a result will be enhanced if we ourselves enter into some new arrangements, perhaps ones that will result in a reduction of our restriction on imports of sugar.

The highly protectionist actions of recent years are now beginning to have adverse effects not only on cereal producers in North America and Australia but on producers in the poor countries as well. Farm policies in the rich countries now have the potential of depriving these countries of the resources they need for development, and this fact is altering the context in which the debate on agricultural policy in Europe, Japan, and elsewhere will take place.

20

Agenda for the 1970's

In preparing an agenda for the 'seventies, one cannot help but note the contrast between the outlook today and that of a decade ago. Thanks to the breakthrough in cereal production, the problems of the 'seventies will be much more political and less technological than were those of the 'sixties. Their solutions lie more in the hands of politicians and less in the hands of scientists and farmers.

Decisions of politicians in the poor countries will, of course, greatly influence the future of the agricultural revolution. But these decisions will not be divorced from the policies and attitudes of the rich countries. "Disengagement" may be possible in specific operations, such as the war in Vietnam, but it is not possible in the case of historic transformations like the agricultural revolution.

One of the great tragedies of the Vietnam war is that it has taken such a toll of humanitarianism in the United States — the humanitarianism that gave us the will, during the years of the Marshall Plan and subsequently, to experiment on a vast scale with international cooperation. The agricultural revolution is perhaps the greatest success story to come out of that period of experimentation. If our unhappy involvement in Vietnam prevents us from pursuing the kinds of adventure that helped to make the agricultural revolution possible, then it will be one of the most terrible tragedies, not only in our own history, but in the history of mankind.

Because of the agricultural revolution, the social and economic problems emphasized in the 'seventies will appear in an entirely new context. The 'seventies can be, if we want to help make them so, much more of a "development decade" than the 'sixties ever were, with an agenda of a much more practical nature than was possible before. The objective that should—and, more important, can—head that agenda is well designed to remove the pall of indifference and disillusion that recently has come to characterize American attitudes toward the world. It can also restore the will and the generosity that made our great contribution to the agricultural revolution possible.

THE ERADICATION OF HUNGER

For the first time in history, it is realistic to consider the eradication of hunger for the overwhelming majority of mankind. Breakthroughs in cereal production and the new food technologies make that a realistic, attainable objective, particularly if the United States were to take the lead in a new worldwide effort. We would be showing the world that we had not lost confidence in ourselves or in those abroad who so desperately need help.

At present, the average diets in the poor countries, which contain more than half of the world's people, are deficient in calories and protein. But enlightened agricultural policies, new food and agricultural technologies, and intelligent employment-creating programs should make it possible to bring the average diet for virtually every country above the nutritional minimum by 1980. This would eliminate most hunger and malnutrition, leaving only fringe groups to be reached by special efforts.

A decision by the United States to provide leadership in a global effort to eradicate hunger is not so ambitious or so inconsistent with previous efforts as it might seem at first. Shortly after World War II, the United States decided that it would use its food resources to avert famine wherever it threatened. As a result, the world has not experienced a massive famine since the one in Bengal in 1943. Even when this policy meant that more of the American wheat crop would be consumed by aid recipients abroad than by the American people at home, as was the case in 1966 and 1967, it was nonetheless rigidly adhered to.

It was not beyond the resources of the American economy to assume the responsibility for avoiding famines. Nor, in the light of today's much greater knowledge and resources, is the goal of eradicating global hunger.

This is not the place to present a detailed strategy for achieving that goal. A useful backdrop for such an effort is provided by the U.N.'s Food and Agriculture Organization in its voluminous *Indicative World Food Plan.* Suffice it to point out here that turning these objectives into an operational plan requires that each country with a nutritional deficit develop a national strategy embodying the entire range of new agricultural and food technologies, including the use of high-yielding, high-protein seeds; more extensive use of fertilizer; the expansion of poultry and livestock industries; the manufacture of high-protein foods from vegetable sources; and fortification of food with vitamins, minerals, and essential amino acids.

The poor countries will need help in fashioning such plans, and the United States is uniquely qualified to provide it. The global research network in agriculture is financed and directed in large part by American foundations, and the largest and best-equipped multinational agribusiness corporations are based in the United States. Furthermore, the United States government employs a greater pool of professional competence in this field than exists in any other country or international organization.

There is no worthier goal for America's international-assistance effort in the 'seventies than the conquest of hunger, and none more urgent—not because hunger is more wide-spread today than in the past, but because it has become so unnecessary. We know how to eliminate the malnutrition that damages brains, dims eyes, and wastes bodies. If we were not able to save Ana Ruth's brother in the situation described in Chapter 15, Ana Ruth herself was saved, and millions more like her can be saved. The eradication of global hunger is an exciting objective, one that the American people can identify with and support with enthusiasm.

Expanding Employment

Eradicating hunger means increasing the over-all supply of food, and we know how to do that. But, as we have seen, it also means expanding employment and raising purchasing power so that food is distributed evenly enough among the population to eradicate hunger.

Employment is the key here. The population explosion makes it certain that the number of young people entering the labor market will rise sharply in the 'seventies. If these entrants have no way of earning an income, they will serve to perpetuate the legacy of hunger and malnutrition.

Finding productive employment for these millions will tax the resources and ingenuity of the poor countries. We would be mistaken to think that Western experience offers clear guidance in this situation. But the rich countries and the poor countries can work together to learn how to create more room in modern society for those who are clamoring for a place. After all, this is a problem common to both rich and poor nations.

We in the United States are not experts on the economics of labor-intensive activities, but this does not mean that we cannot help. In our assistance programs, for example, we can encourage selective farm mechanization and intensive cropping, because both are job-creating activities. At the same time, we can try to discourage the wholesale mechanization that displaces people on a vast scale. We can provide the financing necessary to maintain adequate supplies of fertilizer, and we can help to establish the marketing, credit, and extension services needed to make modern labor-intensive agricultures possible.

Most important, we can adjust our trade policies so that they encourage the momentum of the Green Revolution rather than, as is often the case now, threaten to bring it to a halt. Trade policy should perhaps have pride of place on our agenda for the 'seventies, since trade provides 80 per cent of the foreign exchange available to poor countries. It is also preferable to even the most sensitive assistance program, because it lacks the unpleasant psychological overtones of the aid-donor relationship. It has still another attraction in that export earnings from trade do not have to be repaid as does foreign aid, most of which consists of loans. For these and other reasons, trade is likely to be a source of serious conflict between the rich and poor nations in the 'seventies.

THE RICH-POOR TRADE CONFRONTATION

As surpluses of cereals accumulate in poor countries, there will be increasingly strong political pressures on rich countries to open up their markets to fair competition. Jobs will be at stake, jobs that the poor countries simply cannot afford not to have. Equally important, national pride will be at stake, because if the poor countries are not allowed to earn their way in the markets of the rich when they develop exportable surpluses, they will conclude that the rich countries are attempting to perpetuate the dependent relationship.

The trade confrontation in the 'seventies promises to be much more serious than in the 'sixties. The Kennedy Round of tariff negotiations in the 'sixties was very much of, by, and for the rich countries, paying only lip-service to the needs of the poor countries. In the 'seventies, thanks in large part to the Green Revolution, the bargaining position of the poor countries will be much stronger and their arguments more persuasive. They will also be more militant because so much more will be at stake.

This trend is already becoming apparent. The gathering of Representatives of the 21 Latin American republics assembled at Vina del Mar in May, 1969, produced a unanimous list of demands for American action to correct existing inequities in our economic relationships with our sister republics. This list, presented to President Nixon by the Chilean Ambassador in Washington, was but the first salvo of a battle that promises to dominate international relations in the 'seventies.

A recent remark by President Suharto of Indonesia further indicates the growing tendency of poor countries to challenge the discrepancy between America's rhetoric and its actions in setting national priorities. As President Nixon and his entourage, basking in the light of the Apollo 11 moon landing, were leaving Indonesia, President Suharto, paraphrasing astronaut Neil Armstrong, commented: "A great leap for whom?" He was clearly implying that conditions in Indonesia had not been improved by the accomplishments of the American space program. The human condition in Indonesia had not been bettered in the least.

The confrontation on the question of trade must be put on the agenda simply because it is the inevitable result of historical forces already in motion, the culmination of centuries of evolution in human rights. The poor countries will probably find many more allies among the rich in the 'seventies than they had in the 'sixties. Corporate leaders, bankers, and consumers in the United States and elsewhere are increasingly calling for liberalized trade policies in the national self-interest. As the full cost of trade barriers in agriculture and of discrimination against the poor countries becomes clear to more consumers in the rich countries, and as these barriers add to the inflationary spiral, the possibility emerges of re-enacting debates like that over England's Corn Laws a century and a quarter ago, this time in Europe and Japan. In the United States, sugar could be such an issue. As the number of farmers and related special interests declines in the industrial countries, politicians there will be less willing to ask the consumer to pay high prices to protect uneconomic farm interests; there will be more and more pressure to adopt policies to provide food at the lowest possible cost.

One can imagine, for example, vociferous objection to the policy of setting sugar prices so as to support the beet-sugar industry in the rich countries. Sugar can be produced at such advantage (less than half the cost) in tropical and subtropical climates that it is difficult to justify protecting the beet-sugar producer from international competition. Yet virtually all the rich countries do so. Our own methods of protection are especially capricious. By establishing quotas for several tropical-sugar producers in our markets, designed always to protect beet-sugar growers here at home, we have involved ourselves in the political fortunes of other countries in ways that defy any acceptable definition of national interest. These quotas, set largely by the Congress with the aid of some of the best-paid lawyer-lobbyists in Washington, have had a significant effect on the political development of such countries as Cuba, the Dominican Republic, and the Philippines.

Expanded trade, not only in agricultural products but in labor-intensive manufactures as well, in the long run not only benefits both rich and poor countries but is the only satisfactory alternative to continued financial dependence by the poor. Opening up markets in the rich countries will require new programs to enable those who are inefficient to move more easily into competitive enterprises. Without expanded trade, there is no realistic prospect that enough jobs will be created in the poor countries in the 'seventies to prevent violent social upheavals. Insofar as expanded trade grows out of the Green Revolution itself, it promises to bring greater benefits to the countryside than any amount of financial aid could do. It therefore promises to help balance the distribution of benefits between city and countryside on which the political stability of these countries depends. In no confrontation between rich nations and poor have the stakes been so high.

Sharing the Burdens of Overproduction

Poor countries may find in the 'seventies that they can effectively divide the rich countries in a confrontation over trade policy. Since World War II, the United States has single-handedly assumed responsibility for stabilizing the international market in both wheat and feed grains. With the almost-certain prospect that global overcapacity in these and other cereals will grow in the 'seventies, the time has come to ask whether the American farmer and taxpayer should continue to shoulder this burden alone or whether it might be shared with other rich countries, many of which are now contributing to the surpluses.

At an earlier time, the American economy was the only one with the resources to take productive land out of cultivation in order to prevent gluts on the world market.

Today we divert to nonproductive uses up to 50 million acres, one seventh of our crop land, for just this purpose. The time has come to ask other countries to assume some of the responsibility in the name of carrying forward the agricultural revolution.

The agenda for the 'seventies must include a conference, perhaps convened by the World Bank, of all the rich countries, designed to work out a plan for sharing the excess productive capacity. If the trade confrontation between the rich and the poor is to be resolved constructively, this is a minimal requirement, and an urgent one. While governments have been unwilling to do this until now, the problem is becoming too pressing to delay further. The focus of the conference should be on ways of helping the poor countries to enter world markets with their new agricultural production. The substance of the conference should be a resolution on the part of the rich countries to adopt policies designed to provide food for their people at the lowest price possible.

The mechanics of such a burden-sharing plan would not be difficult. We have had some experience in determining, internationally, the amount of excess acreage that is being planted each year to a given crop. The amount taken out of production could be prorated among the rich countries, perhaps according to some established formula, such as the one used to determine contributions to international organizations like the World Bank and the International Monetary Fund. Diversion of the excess land to recreational, conservational, or other uses could be left up to each country.

Such a conference would test the willingness of the international community in the 'seventies to take a step forward in cooperation comparable to the agreement among the rich countries in the 'sixties to create Special Drawing Rights at the International Monetary Fund. The problem of restructuring world trade in agricultural products is certainly no less urgent for the rich countries, bedeviled as they are by the task of managing inflation without curbing growth. And unlike the agreement creating the SDR's, which so far has not been joined to development of the poor countries, an agreement to share the burdens of excess cereal production would show a renewed interest on the part of the rich in the problems of the poor, as well as one another's problems.

An Example: Japan and the Rice Market

The international rice market provides a good example of the problems and the opportunities involved in trying to share the burden of excess cereal capacity. The world rice market, much smaller than the market for wheat and feed grains, is very sensitive to changes in market conditions. It appears to be headed for a difficult period with the amount of rice available for export at anything approaching a reasonable price almost certain to exceed import needs. The question is what to do about it.

Japan is the only country in a position to avert a major collapse in the world rice market during the 'seventies. It is the only large, high-income country that consumes rice as its staple food. The United States is already holding a sizable portion of its rice acreage out of production and will probably hold back more in the future, but even so we cannot affect the world situation to the same extent as Japan. With an internal support price of $420 per ton—nearly *triple* the current world-market price—Japan is perhaps the most flagrant violator of the laws of comparative advantage of any cereal-producing country. Not only is Japan no longer an importer, but it is now subsidizing exports of rice, thus severely depressing prices in the world market for countries that must make their living from rice exports.

The Japanese rice market, once open to imports from East Asia, is as closed to the outside world today as was Japanese society itself prior to the visit of Admiral Perry a century ago. But rice is the lifeblood of most Asian economies. Should the bottom fall out of the Asian rice market as the cessation of hostilities in Vietnam brings a reduction in the flow of economic resources into the region, development in Southeast Asia could be seriously set back.

Fortunately, several economic factors in Japan today indicate that the policy of raising internal rice prices ever higher may be nearly bankrupt. Inflationary forces, spurred in part by rising rice prices, are becoming stronger. Unemployment is virtually nonexistent and labor shortages are acute. The labor situation could assume crisis proportions owing to the record number of new jobs resulting from a sustained economic growth rate of more than 10 per cent yearly, and to an imminent precipitous decline in the number of young people entering the labor force as a result of a sharp drop in birth rates during the early 'fifties. The alternatives might then be to liberalize farm policies, releasing some of the sizable farm-labor force for non-farm employment, or to import labor from other East Asian countries. One can hope that Japan will opt for the former course.

Japan's great and growing stake in trade and investment in Southeast Asia is also a reason for hoping that Japan can be persuaded to take the lead in sharing the burden of excess rice capacity. The countries of Southeast Asia are precisely the ones that should be exporting rice to Japan, and each currently has a large trade deficit with Japan. This is a classic example of how countries can benefit from trade liberalization. Japanese payment for rice imports from the East Asian countries would enable them to buy more of Japan's industrial products, and Japanese consumers would benefit from cheaper rice.

The United States has little leverage over Japanese policies at this time. We want and need Japan as an active political and eventually military partner in East and Southeast Asia, but the Japanese are warning us that neither is possible in the immediate future. The Japanese are looking for a new relationship with us to replace one that they have come to regard as subservient. Even trade relations between our two countries have become strained as a result.

An appeal to national self-interest might succeed in persuading Japan to share the burden of excess rice capacity. The Japanese do not want to rearm; they would rather conduct their relations with their Asian neighbors by expanding trade and assisting regional development. Japan could make no greater single contribution to these ends than to assume primary responsibility for stabilizing the world rice market. And surely, such a step would serve American and Japanese interests better than pressing Japan to rearm.

REORDERING NATIONAL PRIORITIES

It would be nice to be able to conclude that all that is necessary to sustain the momentum of the agricultural revolution is for the United States to persuade Japan and Europe to shift their priorities away from agricultural protection toward providing food to consumers at the lowest cost. But the weight of the agenda for the 'seventies must rest upon the United States. Many nations are rich enough to follow our lead, but none is rich enough or big enough to take the leadership itself.

The American people are in a period of deep soul-searching. Discussion in the press and in the Congress reflects widespread concern over national priorities. The Vietnam war is just one reason for this concern; the problems of our cities and of our minority groups are the problems of a society that has grown very rich but is still in many ways undeveloped. These are fundamental causes of our discontent.

There seems to be growing consensus that we have been spending too much on "foreign policy" as opposed to "domestic policy." Adherents of this view cite the fact that $82 billion in the current federal budget is appropriated to maintain a vast armed force, to encourage weapons development, and to maintain a network of some 400 military installations abroad. However, it is less well known and more frequently ignored that we are spending only three billion dollars on economic and technical assistance and on food aid. Even this figure is declining. Any reassessment of foreign policy should start with an exploration of the allocation of resources to our role as world policeman as opposed to our role in world development. Insofar as the Vietnam war has blurred the distinction between these two roles, it has made a reassessment of national priorities in the foreign-policy area infinitely more difficult.

We cannot ignore the demands of our security in a turbulent world. But this does not mean spending more; it may mean spending a great deal less. We must begin with some definition of our role in the world that fits our national interests, bearing in mind that it is becoming more and more difficult to separate the national from the global interest. This division of resources must be more consistent with the world as it is in the 'seventies than with the world as it was in the Cold War era, an era that lasted through the 'sixties, long after the Communist monolith as such had ceased to exist.

Our foreign policy, our relations with the world of today, must recognize that the future threat to peace and stability is increasingly Poverty, not Communism. The opportunities to fulfill our role as a participant in world development will be much greater in the 'seventies than in the 'sixties. At the same time, the need to fulfill the policeman's role could be much less, particularly if we fulfill the development role.

In large part, the new opportunities grow out of the agricultural revolution. Just as in the 'sixties we learned how to help others expand food production, so in the 'seventies we can learn to help others create jobs. But this will take more resources for aid, not less.

For many years, the conventional rule for determining a just contribution of public assistance and private investment to world development from the rich countries has been 1 per cent of GNP. The Pearson Commission, in reaffirming this objective, argued that 70 per cent of that contribution should be in the form of official aid. That would require, for the United States, a foreign-aid contribution on the order of eight to ten billion dollars a year by the mid-'seventies, at least double today's level.

There are many ways in which such a contribution could be made: through bilateral programs, multilateral development institutions, trade and investment subsidies, and the like. But these are details. The first question in reordering national priorities in foreign policy should be: Can the United States and the other rich nations continue to progress and prosper in a world in which the gap between rich and poor is rapidly widening, and in which the rich are becoming an ever-smaller minority? Surely the answer can only be no. The problems in the poor countries—hunger, unemployment, technological change, and attendant social turmoil—are sufficiently akin to our own problems to command at least this financial expression of our concern. Perhaps if we had not done so much to master the problems of food production, we could conclude otherwise. But we succeeded, and we must live with our success. Now the clamor for jobs is replacing the clamor for food. If we do not persevere, the successes of the past will be quickly undone.

The breakthrough in cereal production is meaningful because it represents at least the beginning of a solution to the problem of hunger, which until recently was regarded as nearly insoluble. Only a few years ago, it was considered highly unlikely, if not impossible, that most of the additional food needed in the poor countries would be produced within these countries. Farmers were largely illiterate, widely dispersed geographically, and apparently not susceptible to new ideas. Yet the breakthrough occurred. We learned to combine policies and technologies and got agriculture moving.

The problem now is to keep it moving. Otherwise, the farm breakthrough will aggravate the job shortage and accelerate the exodus from the countryside to the already overcrowded cities.

The agricultural breakthrough is significant, not just for itself, but because of the possibility it raises of transferring new techniques and technologies in other areas, such as education and family planning. Recent advances in the rice paddies and wheat fields of the poor countries may usher in a new era in international development as well as in world agriculture.

Thus the new seeds promise to improve the well-being of more people in a shorter time than any other single technological advance in history. They are replacing disappointment and despair with hope. For literally hundreds of millions, they can be the key to the door opening into the twentieth century. But that door will open only if a sustained effort is mounted by the rich and poor countries together.

Selected Bibliography

I. *General*
1. The Pearson Commission, *Partners in Development,* New York: Praeger, 1969.

II. The World Food Problem
1. Lester R. Brown, *Increasing World Food Output,* Washington: Government Printing Office, 1965.
2. Lester R. Brown, *Man, Land and Food,* Washington: Government Printing Office, 1963.
3. Willard W. Cockrane, *The World Food Problem—A Guardedly Optimistic View,* New York: Crowell, 1969.
4. Orville Freeman, *World Without Hunger,* New York: Praeger, 1968.
5. Orville Freeman, "Malthus, Marx and the North American Breadbasket," *Foreign Affairs* (July, 1967).
6. Food and Agriculture Organization of the United Nations, *Provisional Indicative World Plan,* Rome, FAO No. C69/4, August, 1969.
7. Clifford Hardin, ed., *Overcoming World Hunger,* Englewood Cliffs, New Jersey: Prentice-Hall, 1969.
8. President's Science Advisory Committee, *The World Food Problem,* Report of the Panel on the World Food Supply, 3 vols., Washington, Government Printing Office, 1967.
9. Rockefeller Foundation, *Strategy for the Conquest of Hunger,* proceedings of a symposium convened by the Rockefeller Foundation at the Rockefeller University, April, 1968.
10. E. C. Stakman, Richard Bradfield, and Paul C. Mangelsdorf, *Campaigns Against Hunger,* Cambridge: Belknap Press of Harvard University Press, 1967.

III. Agricultural Development
1. Asian Development Bank, *Asian Agricultural Survey,* Tokyo: University of Tokyo Press, 1969; Seattle: University of Washington Press, 1969.
2. Asian Studies Center, *Development and Change in Traditional Agriculture: Focus on South Asia,* East Lansing: Michigan State University, 1968.

197

3. Lester R. Brown, "The Agricultural Revolution in Asia," *Foreign Affairs,* July, 1968.

4. Theodore W. Schultz, *Economic Growth and Agriculture,* New York: McGraw-Hill, 1968.

5. Clifton R. Wharton, Jr., "The Green Revolution: Cornucopia or Pandora's Box?" *Foreign Affairs,* April, 1969.

6. Montague Yudelman, *Agricultural Development in Latin America: Current Status and Prospects,* Inter-American Development Bank, Washington, 1966.

IV. High-yielding Varieties and Associated Technologies

    1. Asian Productivity Organization, *Expert Group Meeting on Agricultural Mechanization,* Vol. II, APO, Tokyo, 1968.

    2. R. Barker, S. H. Liao, and S. K. DeDatta, *Economic Analysis of Rice Production from Experimental Results to Farmer Fields,* paper presented at Agronomy Department Seminar, UPCA, Philippines, IRRI, 1968.

    3. Dana Dalrymple, *Technological Changes in Agriculture,* U.S. Department of Agriculture, Foreign Agricultural Service, cooperating with Agency for International Development, Washington, 1969.

    4. Dana Dalrymple, *Imports and Plantings of High-Yielding Varieties of Wheat and Rice in the Less Developed Nations,* mimeographed, U.S. Department of Agriculture, International Agricultural Development Service, Washington, 1968.

    5. John K. Frizzel, *The Performance of Mexican Wheat in Turkey, 1967–1968,* mimeographed, U.S. Agency for International Development, Ankara.

    6. L. M. Humphrey, *Mexican Wheat Comes to Turkey,* Food and Agriculture Division, U.S. AID/Turkey, 1969.

    7. Indian Agricultural Research Institute, *Five Years of Research on Dwarf Wheats,* IARI, New Delhi, 1968.

    8. International Rice Research Institute, *The Seminar-Workshop on the Economics of Rice Production,* papers presented at a conference at the International Rice Research Institute, December, 1967.

    9. International Rice Research Institute, *Annual Report, 1966,* IRRI, Los Banos, Laguna, Philippines, 1966.

    10. International Rice Research Institute, *Annual Report, 1967,* IRRI, Los Banos, Lagua, Philippines, 1967.

    11. Joseph W. Willett, *The Impact of New Varieties of Rice and Wheat in Asia,* paper presented at the Spring Review of the Agency for International Development, Washington, 1969.

V. Country Studies

    1. L. Jay Atkinson, *Changes in Agricultural Production and Technology in Colombia,* Economic Research Service, United

States Department of Agriculture in cooperation with the Ministry of Agriculture and Central Planning of Colombia, FAER No. 52, Washington, June, 1969.

2. Raymond P. Christensen, *Taiwan's Agricultural Development: Its Relevance for Developing Countries Today*, No. 39, U.S. Department of Agriculture, Washington, 1968.

3. Walter P. Falcon and Carl H. Gotsch, *Agricultural Development in Pakistan: Lessons from the Second Plan Period*, Economic Development Report No. 6, presented at the D.A.S. Conference, Bellagio, Italy: Center for International Affairs, Harvard University, 1966.

4. William E. Hendrix, *Approaches to Agricultural Development in India, 1949–1965*, draft report prepared for Ministry of Food, Agriculture, Community Development and Cooperation, Government of India, U.S. Agency for International Development and Economic Research Service, USDA, 1969.

5. Reed Hertford, *The Measured Sources of Growth of Mexican Agricultural Production and Productivity*, draft report, U.S. Department of Agriculture, Economic Research Service, Washington, 1968.

6. George Mehren, *Needs and Opportunities for Private Investment in the Agricultural Economy of West Pakistan*, New York: Agribusiness Council, September, 1969.

7. John Mellor, Thomas Wearer, Uma Lele, and Sheldon Simon, *Developing Rural India*, Ithaca: Cornell University Press, 1968.

VI. International Technology, Business, and Trade

1. Aaron Altschul, "Using Unused Protein Supplies," *IAD Newsletter*, International Agricultural Development Service, U.S. Department of Agriculture, February, 1968.

2. J. R. Barse, *Japan's Food Demand and 1985 Food Grain Imports*, USDA Foreign Agricultural Economic Report No. 53, Government Printing Office, Washington, June 1969.

3. I. M. Destler, "Ecological Imbalance—Man's Pressure on the Land," *IAD Newletter*, International Agricultural Development Service, U.S. Department of Agriculture, February 1968.

4. R. E. Friend and G. R. Butell, *Production, Consumption and Trade of Coarse Grains*, USDA Economic Research Service — Foreign 272, June, 1969.

5. Raymond Ewell, *Fertilizer Outlook—Domestic, Short Term*, paper presented at Annual Convention of National Plant Food Institute, The Greenbrier, White Sulphur Springs, West Virginia, June, 1968.

6. Harald B. Malmgren and David L. Schlechty, *Technology and Neo-Mercantilism in International Agricultural Trade*,

paper presented at annual meeting of American Agricultural Economics Association, Lexington, Kentucky, August 18, 1969.

7. J. J. Servan-Schreiber, *The American Challenge*, New York: Atheneum, 1968.

8. Tennessee Valley Authority, *Estimated World Fertilizer Production Capacity as Related to Future Needs 1967 to 1972–80*, Muscle Shoals, Alabama, 1968.

9. Quentin M. West, *The Future for U.S. Grain Exports*, paper presented at the Transportation-Distribution Symposium of the Grain and Feed Dealers National Association, New Orleans, January 1969.

Index

Abortion, 131
ADT-27 (wheat), 21
Afghanistan: crop-production campaign in, 9; Mexican wheat in, 19, 22; rice production in, 5; self-sufficiency in, 158; yield takeoff in, 38, 40
Agency for International Development (AID), 8, 26, 67, 69, 132
Agricultural Guarantee Loan Fund, in the Philippines, 96
Agricultural protectionism, 176–81
Agricultural reform, 110–17
Agricultural Research Service, U.S. Department of Agriculture, 69
Agriculture, U.S. Department of, 8
Algeria, wheat production in, 5
American farmer, 167–75
Amino acids, 145–46
Ammonia process, for fertilizers, 56–57

Bacon substitute, 151
Bananas, protein content of, 141
Bell, David, 69
Berg, Alan, 149
Birth rate, prospects of reduction of, 129–32
Borlaug, Norman, 17
Boulware, James, 87
Brazil: exportable surpluses in, 160; fertilizers in, 57, 59–60; wheat production in, 5
Brunthaver, Carroll G., 171
Burma: agricultural research in, 51; rice production in, 5; yield takeoff in, 38

Byrnes, Frank, 136–37

Cassava, protein content of, 141
Cereal staples, self-sufficiency in, 158
Cereals, production of, 140
Ceylon: agricultural research in, 51; multiple cropping in, 33; rice production in, 5, 140; self-sufficiency in, 157, 158; wheat and rice production trends in, 39; wheat production in, 21; yield takeoff in, 38, 40
Chandler, Robert, 4, 18
Chile, land reform in, 113
Common Market, 177
Consolidated farming, 114–16
Consumer resistance, 93–94
Contraceptives, 131
Corn, protein content of, 141

Demirel, Suleiman, 9
Deo-geo-woo-gen (rice), 18
Diversification, 160–63
Dry-season farming, 31–32
Dwarf rice, 4, 18, 22, 24
Dwarf wheat, 16–17, 20

East Pakistan: farm income in, 41–42; irrigation system in, 28; regional disparities in, 80; yield takeoff in, 38; see also Pakistan; West Pakistan
Ehrlich, Paul, 135
Employment, expanding of, 185–86
Employment-population equation, 122–26